Hope and Education

This book is a rallying cry to teachers at a time when many in the pro-fession feel profoundly pessimistic about their work and the future of education. In this uplifting book, David Halpin suggests ways of put-ting the hope back into education, exploring the value of and need for utopian thinking in discussions of the purposes of education and the direction of school policy.

David Halpin does not attempt to predict the future of schooling. Rather, he discusses the attitude educators should adopt about its reform and the prospect of educational change. He suggests that educa-tors need to adopt a militant optimism of the will, applying aspects of the utopian imagination through which hopefulness can be brought to bear on educational situations.

This important book will stimulate fresh thinking about school reform. It will be interesting reading for those studying for Masters and Doctoral degrees in education and academics, researchers and policy-makers working in the same field.

David Halpin is Professor of Education and Head of the School of Curriculum, Pedagogy and Assessment at the Institute of Education, University of London. He is also Editor of *The London Review of Education*.

Hope and Education
The role of the utopian imagination

David Halpin

RoutledgeFalmer
Taylor & Francis Group

LONDON AND NEW YORK

First published 2003
by RoutledgeFalmer
11 New Fetter Lane, London EC4P 4EE

Simultaneously published in the USA and Canada
by RoutledgeFalmer
29 West 35th Street, New York, NY 10001

RoutledgeFalmer is an imprint of the Taylor & Francis Group

© 2003 David Halpin

Typeset in Sabon by BC Typesetting, Bristol
Printed and bound in Great Britain by
Biddles Ltd, Guildford and King's Lynn

British Library Cataloguing in Publication Data
A catalogue record for this book is available from the British Library

Library of Congress Cataloging in Publication Data

ISBN 0–415–23367–4 (hbk)
ISBN 0–415–23368–2 (pbk)

For Chloe and Jacob, my two utopias

Contents

Preface and acknowledgements

This book is the outcome of two lines of thought which have pre-occupied me as a public educator for as many years as I can remember, and certainly long before I became a university teacher and researcher in 1987. One of these is a standing concern with issues to do with the relationship between theory and practice in education; the other is an abiding interest in the interplay between professional commitment and political praxis in the same context. These lines first came to prominence in my thinking as I grappled with questions of what kind of teacher I wanted to be when I first joined the profession in the 1970s, at which time I was very active politically – chiefly within the National Union of Teachers (UK) and the British Labour Party.

Thirty-two years later, they intersect in this book at the junction between hope and utopianism, and in the working out of what both might mean for rethinking and re-evaluating my own work and that of teachers generally at a time when there is considerable uncertainty about what this should entail and with what it should be centrally concerned.

The book in fact began life as a lecture – specifically, an inaugural professorial lecture (*Utopian Ideals, Democracy and the Politics of Education*) which I gave as Research Professor of Education at Goldsmiths College, University of London, on 29 April 1997. In that lecture I rehearsed for the first time arguments about the value of utopian thinking for social and educational reform, some of which are repeated, but developed further, in the pages that follow. I am grateful to the authorities at Goldsmiths for permission to reuse parts of that lecture in this book, as I am to David Hockney for approving the use of his oil painting *Sunflowers for Hope and Joy* (November, 1995) in its cover design.

I am also grateful to the Editors of the following academic journals for permission to quote from and rework other previously published material of mine: *Journal of Education Policy* ('Utopian realism and a new politics of education: developing a critical theory without guarantees', which appeared in Vol. 14, No. 4, 1999, pp. 345–61); *Cambridge Journal of Education* ('Hope, utopianism and educational management', Vol. 31, No. 1, 2001, pp. 103–18); *International Journal of Inclusive Education* ('Democracy, inclusive schooling and the politics of education', Vol. 3, No. 3, 1999, pp. 225–38); *Oxford Review of Education* ('Maintaining, reconstructing and creating tradition in education' [co-authored with A. Moore], Vol. 26, No. 2, 2000, pp. 133–44); *Forum* ('Sociologising the third way: the contribution of Anthony Giddens and the significance of his analysis for education', Vol. 41. No. 2, 1999, pp. 53–7); *British Journal of Educational Studies* ('Utopianism and education: the legacy of Thomas More', Vol. 49, No. 3, 2001, pp. 299–315; 'The nature of hope and its significance for education', Vol. 49, No. 4, 2001, pp. 392–410) and *School Leadership and Management* ('Education action zones and democratic participation' [co-authored with M. Dickson, S. Power, S. Gewirtz, G. Whitty and D. Telford], Vol. 21, No. 2, 2001, pp. 169–81).

Special thanks are also due to the pupils, staff and headteacher of Bishop Challoner School in Birmingham who provided me with the data which led to the writing of the exemplary case study of utopian school leadership that features strongly in Chapter 5.

I owe equal debts of gratitude to a number of colleagues and friends, each of whom, in different ways, tutored my judgement for the better about particular parts of the book. They include Harry Brighouse and Gwyn Edwards, each of whom commented critically on my interpretation of the value of utopianism; Geoff Whitty, Sally Power, Sharon Gewirtz and Marny Dickson, who together aided my understanding of area-based approaches to school improvement and educational reform; Alex Moore and Rosalyn George, who helped to clarify my thinking about the nature of tradition and the role it plays in education; Gerald Grace, who prompted me to develop further my discussion of Thomas More's legacy; and Alan Day and Patrick Eavis, who each offered editorial advice on earlier versions of particular chapters. While I have not always taken these people's advice, I am grateful to them for offering it, not least on those occasions when it convinced me that my analysis was better than they judged, which means of course I am ultimately responsible for whatever faults other people now detect in it.

I am enormously indebted too to Kathryn Brownridge for the general support she provided as I struggled to complete the book's first draft.

Finally, I want to say a big 'thank you' for the patience and excellent editorial guidance offered by the book's publisher, RoutledgeFalmer, in particular Anna Clarkson, its Senior Commissioning Editor who kept faith with me as I missed deadline after deadline, and Ann King who copyedited the manuscript so brilliantly.

Introduction

> Hope is the knowledge that we can choose; that we can learn from our
> mistakes and act differently next time.
>
> (Jonathan Sacks)

> In utopia there is the hope of a better society. In hope there is the utopia
> of a different world.
>
> (Henri Desroche)

The purpose of this book is to offer an analysis of the nature of hope
and its utopian counterpart, and to explain their joint significance for
the practice of education. The book is aimed at serious-minded educators – chiefly teachers studying for a higher degree in education and
other education professionals who are looking for a fresh way of reinterpreting the significance of their work in order both to retain and
renew a sense of optimism about and commitment to it. It is most
definitely not a book for the restricted educational professional, nor
is it one for teachers seeking practical tips for the classroom.

Although short on specific advice, the book's theories about educational practice, if found compelling, have profound consequences for
thinking anew about the nature of teaching, learning and management
and governance in schools. These theories about educational practice
explore questions concerning the present value of, and need for,
utopian thinking in discussions of the purposes of education and
policy to meet the challenges of the new millennium. They also suggest
a way of putting the hope back into the education process at a time
when many teachers in schools are despairing of their work and feeling
profoundly pessimistic about it as a result.

Although a utopia about utopianism in the education context, this
book does not attempt to predict the future of schooling. Rather, it

discusses the kind of attitude educators should consider having about its reform and about the prospect of educational change generally. Basically, this attitude is one that entails the adoption of a militant optimism of the will in the course of which a form of *ultimate hope* is brought to bear on educational situations and problems through specific applications of the utopian imagination.

Like many of the ideas in this book, the expression *ultimate hope* is not my own, but one borrowed from the existential philosopher Gabriel Marcel, whose work on the subject is central to Joseph Godfrey's (1987) general theory of hope. As will become clear, Godfrey's discussion of Marcel's work has influenced very much my own view of the role played by hope in matters to do with education and change. As its mode of expression suggests, *ultimate hope* is not to be confused with wistful yearning. On the contrary, in Godfrey's schema, *ultimate hope* is 'aimed hope', entailing social objectives and, relatedly, a 'core of trust'. Moreover, its focus is 'on hope when there is obstacle, when the one who hopes cares a great deal, and when a great deal is at stake' (1987, p. 14). Such hope, it will be argued, is particularly applicable to the practice of education. Indeed, one of my aims in writing this book is to encourage in those who read it new forms of hopefulness in education through an appreciation of its relevance to thinking progressively about teaching and learning and management and governance in schools.

In undertaking this task I want to show how utopianism can play a special and significant part in bolstering and encouraging *ultimate hope* in education. So, while I am fully aware of the indifferent historic reputation of some utopias and utopians, I will insist that, currently, we need new utopian visions in education (as well as elsewhere), not their abandonment. To that extent, I subscribe to Milan Simecka's assessment that a world without utopias 'would be a world without social hope – a world of resignation to the status quo' (1984, p. 175). Indeed, it seems to me that, on those occasions when it is not a means of legitimizing satisfaction with the social and political status quo, attacks on utopianism are about as meaningful as denunciations of dreaming. Krishan Kumar goes further, arguing that utopian conceptions are 'indispensable to politics and to progress; without them, politics is a soulless world, a mere instrumentality without purpose or vision' (1991, p. 95). I agree with that. I concur too with Oscar Wilde's (1894) earlier view that 'a map of the world that does not include utopia is not worth even glancing at, for it leaves out the one country at which humanity is always landing' (1986, p. 34). Wilde's suggestion that the pursuit of utopia requires us to embark on a kind of journey represents well the spirit in which I have approached the writing of this book, to the extent that it should be read more as an explorative argument than a polished, all-written-up and original contribution to the history of ideas in education.

This book has no pretence either to be a work of primary scholarship since, as will become quickly apparent, its arguments are heavily dependent upon a host of secondary sources, of which Godfrey's work is just one example. No one with a life of finite duration could expect to be an expert on the entire *oeuvre* of figures that over the centuries have contributed to the massive literature on utopia and utopianism. Consequently, I have unashamedly drawn on a host of recent and not so recent reviews of the genre as well as commentaries on its history, nature, role and function. These are all acknowledged in the text. In addition, I have mined extensively the work of certain contemporary social theorists in the course of developing other aspects of the book's analysis, notably that produced by Anthony Giddens (on 'structuration theory', 'globalization', 'post-traditionalism', 'dialogic democracy' and the 'Third Way'), Ulrich Beck (on the 'risk society' and 'new individualism') and Zygmunt Bauman (on 'culture'). I have also sought to engage critically with a variety of other very influential arguments that I consider not only antithetical to utopianism, but wrong and dangerous generally. Chief among these are those viewpoints which have their origins within a postmodern framework, the self-congratulatory cynical pessimism of which I regard as one of the main enemies of *ultimate hope*.

Discourses about hope that stress social aims and progress are generally frowned upon by postmodernists because they imply that universal or foundational truths are both discoverable and applicable as guidelines for political action, something which they deny is either possible or necessary. Intellectuals of a postmodernist persuasion view such suggestions as the chief sins of the so-called 'Enlightenment project', and of the 'totalizing' and 'homogenizing' modernism it supposedly generated. In their place, they offer us a world devoid of 'grand narratives' – 'a life without truths, standards and ideals' (Bauman, 1992, p. ix) – in which we must take up positively the challenge of thorough going scepticism. Indeed, such a life has no 'outside' as such, happiness within it being gained by 'saying yes to transience' and by 'making a friend of the void'. For some postmodernists there is consequently no need to anticipate a future because the future is here already, in the shape of a perversely idealized world of 'anything goes' – a world I regard as profoundly dystopian, and thus to be avoided and challenged.

Having written that, I need to state quickly that there is an obvious sense in which some aspects of postmodern scepticism are not only proper, but imperative, especially in those circumstances today in which people are the victims of particular forms of totalizing discourse – crude nationalism arguably being the most potent example at the moment. But, equally, meaningful political action, both generally and in the education context in particular, cannot surely proceed without some embedded sense of value? Moreover, whatever some post-modernists may say to the contrary, no one can doubt everything at the same time and expect to think on, let alone act with a purpose. Accordingly, like David Harvey, I see the essential task of critical analysis as not about proving 'the impossibility of foundational beliefs or truths, but [rather about finding] a more plausible and adequate basis for the foundational beliefs that make interpretation and political action meaningful, creative and possible' (1996, p. 2). In any event, if foundationalism of this sort is said to be over and done with, one has to ask why there is still so much of it around – or why, to paraphrase Terry Eagleton, 'does the good news of the end of ideology appear to have successfully seeped through to Berkeley and Bologna, but not to Utah or Ulster?' (1996, p. 19).

Even if it had, a world in which 'anything goes' would surely be all right only as long as everyone accepted that this was so. But this is a dangerous fantasy, for the reality would be that some people in such a world would abuse the liberty of 'anything goes' to impose their own views, certain of which would be simply intolerable. Thus, as the political theorist Paul Hirst enjoins us,

> we cannot abandon the search for specific standards of validity as if they were no more than an old-fashioned 19th century positivist illusion, out of date in a world of multiple perspectives and the creative use of whatever discursive resources we please . . . *Validity is as much a political issue as it is an intellectual one, for what beliefs are taken as valid [or foundational] determines the whole tenor of the social order.*
>
> (1993, p. 59, emphasis added)

The search for such standards cannot be undertaken satisfactorily for its own sake, however. Rather, its ultimate purpose is not to do with winning an argument but with constructing a pragmatic response, which in the case of this book is about contributing positively to the creation of a consensus on the best ends to be achieved in education and the most effective means to realize them.

In wishing to engage in this sort of deliberative process, I am clear about my own priorities, which ultimately are to do with identifying, and fostering agreement about, those principles of procedure and action plans that contribute to the creation of a more equal and more democratic education system and society.

I am clear too that such pragmatism will never realize anything more than a series of appropriate temporary settlements, which assist for the moment, while the search goes on for even better solutions to our problems. To that extent I follow the American pragmatist philosopher, Richard Rorty, who argues that 'a perfected society will not live up to a pre-existent standard, but (instead) will be an artistic achievement, produced by the same long and difficult process of trial and error as is required by any other creative effort' (1999, p. 270).

The cultural historian Raymond Williams described this process as the 'long revolution' which, for him, was centrally about an extended effort to implement better and more equal patterns of economic and political association. While it is clear that the exertion of effort in this direction must, by definition, include both success and failure, the process itself is always about 'framing new expectations in terms of a *continuing* version of what life could be like' (Williams, 1965, p. 380) – in other words, in terms of a utopian vision of a better society.

Postmodernism's mockery at the possibility of social progress along such lines, and its scornful dismissal of the idea that specific standards of validity are worth searching for is likely to be self-fulfilling if we are not careful. Certainly, if we do not believe in the possibility of a specific better future for society and for its educational institutions – brought about by progressive and patient incremental social reform – that future will surely not come about. Indeed, to my way of thinking, public intellectuals have a special responsibility to those who otherwise might be without it to keep alive the hope of progress of this kind. Williams, to whose words I had recourse a moment ago, once argued in a similar way, proclaiming that intellectuals have a duty to 'speak for hope'. In the same sentence, however, he urged them to do so in ways that do not 'suppress the nature of the danger' (1989, p. 322), by which he meant the need for them to couch their hopes for the future in terms that take adequately into account the actual social context for their effective implementation.

This approach to bringing about change connects well with Rorty's (1998) advice to those currently on the political Left that they should become more modest with regard to revolution and more fervent with reform. In particular, and significantly given the purposes of this book, he urges them to abandon the search for naive utopias, favouring in its place the reinvention of a realistic, but none the less radical politics of hope (p. 14). Terry Eagleton says much the same in the course of distinguishing between 'good' and 'bad' utopias. The latter, he says, 'consist simply in a sort of wistful yearning, a "wouldn't it be nice if", with no basis in the actual'. The former, on the other hand, 'finds a bridge between present and future in those forces within the present which are potentially able to transform it' (2000b, p. 22).

In writing this book I have wanted not only to take on particular ideas which I find disturbingly mistaken. I have also wished to react to and counter an intellectual and political tendency I consider a hindrance to the aim of seeking out imaginative practical solutions to enduring social difficulties. Unlike the postmodernist attitude that celebrates the plurality of ideas, and the consequent fragmentation of perspectives, this tendency takes the form of gross dissension and the polarization of opinion in the course of which people of differing views become effectively deaf to each other. It is a tendency that implicitly subscribes to the fatuity of there being just 'one side to every question', not a multiplicity of fascinating facets or ones not yet thought of. It is a mode of deliberation that results in some people propagating only the one version of events that best suits their own position; a version which is contrasted positively with all other ones, which are routinely castigated in the process – a form of argumentation that Ulrich Beck (1997) graphically refers to as the politics of 'Either-Or'.

Among other things, this form of political deliberation within education alleges: either state monopoly or privatization; either comprehensive schooling or selection; either setting or mixed-ability teaching; either single-sex education or co-education. As this list indicates, 'either-or' politics in the education context take in a host of disparate issues and concerns. Their 'either-or' nature, of course, is largely due to the fact that many aspects of education are profoundly value-laden, making it an area of public life that inevitably attracts comment of a politically partisan nature and therefore one that is easily politicized as a result. Indeed, people who are highly politically motivated often self-consciously use education as a key site for their personal ideological struggles and justify their partisan attitudes about it by reference to its alleged inevitably political character. The trouble with this position, however, is that it tends to assume that all, or most, important issues about education are necessarily political, when arguably some are not, other than in an indirect sense, such as, for example, how best to help young children to begin to learn to read. While such matters clearly have cultural, evaluative even, aspects, to insist they are necessarily 'political' is possibly to stretch our understanding of that word in a direction that either renders it almost empty of significant sense or trivializes its meaning.

Moreover, the intrusion of the overtly political in debates about education policy can sometimes lead to a failure to consider fairly particular models for reform because their brand-names are ideologically ruled out by definition. The Left's knee-jerk rejection of the role of the private sector in providing school services is a case in point, despite the fact that some kinds of privatisation in education may be perfectly compatible with its conceptions of social justice (Brighouse, 2003, forthcoming).

The historic impact of particular 'either-or' proposals for educational reform, which entails a curious mix of apparent success in one place and dismal failure in another, suggests that their proponents may also be guilty of over-simplifying the problems they seek to address. It may be the case too that the problems are themselves resistant to solutions that embody imperatives which are ideologically inflected in one dimension only.

Sadly, a significant aspect of the process of commending such solutions by those who propose them is often the hostile denigration of oppositional alternatives, entailing what Stephen Ball (1990) has described vividly as a distinctive 'discourse of derision'. Although his analysis associates this discursive attitude with the political Right, it is arguably practised as well, and with equal effect, by Left education intellectuals. Thus described, the process mimics what Deborah Tannen (1998) suggests is a dominant feature of contemporary argument generally – the dismissal of other people's suggestions as a first, sometimes only, line of defence of one's own. It also denies the possibility that out of debate will come progress rather than the victory of one side over another.

By contrast, the politics of 'And-Also' (Follett, 1926, Kadinsky, 1982), which later on in this book I will strongly associate with a utopian attitude defined as 'utopian realism', eschews such bipolarisms by seeking out instead integrated solutions to problems instead of unilateral ones. These solutions derive less from the extremes of political analysis and more from a strategic mix of genuinely experimental ideas whose ideological derivation is neither here nor there, but *which connect meaningfully with what is judged to be actually happening in society*. While this mode of political pragmatism – sometimes called the *Third Way* – is clearly value-based, it is not ideologically driven in the way that, for example, Marxism and neo-Liberalism are, each of which exhibits strong exclusionary characteristics which the former seeks to move beyond. Utopianism is similarly positioned inasmuch as it does not necessarily belong to a definite ideology, but rather often occupies a sort of neutral limitless place within the 'gap' between opposite terms, something about which I will also say more later on.

This does mean, however, that deliberation about key aspects of the education process which takes seriously a utopian starting point results in education ceasing altogether to be regarded as a political project. On the contrary, one of the aims of this book is to commend utopianism as one means of finding a new politics of education that is differently political to the ways to which most of us have grown used – one that side-steps earlier antagonisms in favour of a new pragmatic eclecticism. Accordingly, this book does not seek to depoliticize education but, instead, outlines a way to *repoliticize* it in a manner that avoids commitment to any existing universe of fixed, or near-fixed, set of categories. My chief aim, however, is to describe the way in which specific applications of the utopian imagination have the capacity to project a measure of *ultimate hope* into deliberations about educational reform – one that can act as a spur to action as well as give direction to it.

Utopia's capacity to work this effect derives from three features of its usual mode of expression. On the one hand, it is always configured positively, and in such a way which forces us to consider the idea that, despite present difficulties and past disappointments, an improved way of life can be realized, if not in the immediate here and now, then certainly in the foreseeable future. On the other hand, utopias usually embody a radical political outlook by holding up to critical scrutiny old certainties in favour of new, albeit often unsettling, portrayals of a better future. Their radicalism, however, is not necessarily expressed in terms that are immediately recognizable as being of either the political Left or Right. Finally, while they often stress ends at the expense of considering the means to achieve them, many, even theoretical, utopias are realistically grounded in actual social processes or based upon a critique of their existing limitations.

Being hopeful, radical and realistic are powerful motivational forces. Moreover, they have a special salience in the education context at the moment because many of its aspects are frequently experienced and spoken about negatively. Today, increasing numbers of people are justifiably sceptical of, sometimes even cynical about, official solutions to educational problems which appear permanently resistant to particular kinds of reform. The sorts of problem I have chiefly in mind here are those to do with student underachievement and underperforming schools; the sorts of solution that entail making adjustments to the prevailing infrastructure of educational provision. Applying the utopian imagination to such problems, it will be argued, can lead to very different outcomes. Certainly, by facilitating the process of temporarily putting to one side our assumptions about the existing order of things, and the current supposed limits of change, it assists the development of radical, previously untried and potentially success-ful policies for education. Interpreted in this way, utopianism provides a justification for considering the previously inconceivable without fear of embarrassment or premature contradiction. As such, it offers some relief from the undermining influence of fatalism and cynicism, and the corrosive effect of excessive scepticism and debilitating forms of pessimism.

This book is divided into:

- *Chapter 1* which discusses the nature of hope and explores its significance for education.
- *Chapter 2* which introduces utopianism as a literary genre and way of thinking, pointing up its potential for providing a distinctive vocabulary of hope in the education context.
- *Chapter 3* which develops the analysis of utopianism by looking in detail at one example of it – Thomas More's *Utopia* – which is used to illustrate further how applications of the utopian imagination can have profound consequences for the way in which we think about the practice of education and its reform.
- *Chapter 4* which discusses a particular version of the utopian imagination – *utopian realism* – which is connected subsequently to an approach to developing a so-called *Third Way* for political action in the education context.
- *Chapters 5, 6* and *7* which examine how the perspective of utopian realism can be usefully applied respectively to three key areas of education policy and practice: the management and leadership of schools; the governance of schooling; and the aims and content of a reformed compulsory 'core' curriculum for general education in schools.
- *Chapter 8* which outlines briefly a series of 'signposts' which offer some direction to putting the hope back into education.

1 Hope and its significance for education

Teaching . . . is in every respect a profession of hope.

(Vito Perrone)

A story from the field

If some of the stories emanating from the field are to be believed, teaching is presently a beleaguered occupation, particularly in schools serving areas of cumulative social and economic disadvantage. Many teachers working in such settings are reported to have low morale, coupled, in some cases, with feelings of professional inadequacy. Indeed, a recent study conducted by a group of economists at the University of Warwick UK (Gardner and Oswald, 1999) suggests that teachers in England are less content at work than any other professional group.

The factors contributing to this state of affairs are not difficult to identify. Teaching in urban environments, while it has its obvious rewards, can often be grindingly hard. Certainly teachers in many of our inner-city state comprehensive schools are required to work with the most challenging of students, in situations that are often less than ideal, and in circumstances in which they feel their efforts are insufficiently acknowledged and inadequately rewarded.

Here is how one of them – a 46-year old male – described his work in an article that appeared in the *Times Educational Supplement* a few years ago:

> I work with 14-year old children who have 39-year old grandparents, whose families are fourth or fifth generation unemployed and whom the police deem 'out of control'. Many started their sex lives at 12 and already smoke and drink heavily. We manage and they pass some exams, but they won't get jobs because there aren't

any. I don't have carpet in any room I work in and the furniture is broken. I don't even work in the same room all the time. My office is a chair in the staff room and I don't have a personal phone or computer terminal. The windows and roof leak. Bright displays cover holes in the walls. It is cold in winter and too hot in summer. The building is unhealthy, badly designed and, until recently, full of asbestos. Some of my classes have more than 30 children, all of which have a right to individual attention and some of which have special needs. I haven't had a full set of textbooks in years and produce photocopies and worksheets in my own time. If children misbehave, it is apparently my fault for inadequate child-management skills. I have been hectored by the press, badgered by parents, pressured by management, and insulted by politicians, just for being a teacher. . . . I've worked through innumerable Secretaries of State for Education, and I feel that I can wear my despair and cynicism as the professional equivalent of a long service and good conduct medal. I have earned a privileged insight into my job the hard way and – unlike some politicians – I know exactly what I am talking about. I am a good teacher because I appreciate and like children. I enjoy my subject, and I admire learning, but I am going to need a lot of help to trust a politician again. The Government and my management will have to support me in order to get back some of the loyalty and sense of vocation that has been squandered need-lessly. The years to retirement are going to be a long, hard haul and if I could leave teaching, I'd go tomorrow. . . . *I'm not sure I have much hope or faith left.*

(*TES*, 6 November 1998, p. 13, emphasis added)

This almost entirely negative assessment by one teacher of his work circumstances, of course, needs to be read critically alongside others that portray things altogether differently and more positively. On the other hand, if the comments the article elicited in the letter columns of subsequent editions of the *Times Educational Supplement* are any guide, its description of the experience of what it is like today to be a secondary schoolteacher is one shared by many others in similar posi-tions. Thus, while it reports a single case, parts of the account are shockingly recognizable.

The large amount of discontent said to permeate teaching is one reason, I suspect, why today fewer of its practitioners than in previous times think of it as a job for life. Indeed, a high number do not even start out. Figures issued by the UK's Teacher Training Agency three years ago, for example, point up the disappointing extent to which graduates who are completing programmes of teacher training increasingly do not seek teaching posts (Smithers, 1999). For those who do, a high 'drop-out' rate after five years is evident. It appears too that more and more experienced teachers, including many occupying senior posts, are actively seeking ways to retire early, often because of stress in the workplace. (In this connection, figures recently issued by the UK government indicate that nearly half of all teachers working in state schools in England in 2001 were compelled to take four or more weeks off work because of work-related illness. In addition, there are other data which suggest that currently up to 5,000 UK teachers retire each year on grounds of ill-health compared with about 2,000 in 1990.) So, although cynicism and pessimism are probably not as widespread among teachers in England as some might think, it remains the case that neither optimism nor hopefulness is present in super-abundance either.

But what is meant by hope in general and how does it connect with the educational process in particular? Neither question is easy to answer, for while it is clear that vocabularies of hope crucially affect people's thinking, emotions and achievements, and perhaps teachers' more than most, hope itself has rarely been at the centre of detailed theoretical attention or intensive empirical investigation. My own search for relevant literature in the course of writing this book, for instance, brought to light only a handful of comprehensive accounts of its nature and significance (namely, Dauenhauer, 1986; Godfrey, 1987; Kast, 1991; Ludema, 2000; Ludema *et al.*, 1997; Lynch, 1965). As Godfrey observes, 'as a topic for study, hope has largely been left to psychologists and theologians. For the most part, philosophers treat [it] *en passant*' (1987, p. xi). It is also a neglected concept in the academic study of education.

Hope as a theological virtue

One of the *historic* roots of hopefulness is Christian theology – specifically, Pauline ethics. Saint Paul, in one of his letters to the Christian Church in Corinth, identified hope, along with faith and love, as one of the three 'theological virtues'. Drawing on the ethical philosophy of Aristotle, Saint Thomas Aquinas (1952, II, I: 62), developing this insight, articulated Saint Paul's taxonomy with one of his own – the four 'cardinal or moral virtues' of temperance, justice, prudence and fortitude, the latter of which he conceived as the necessary means for bringing about the former.

Aquinas' ancient cardinal virtues have much to teach us about the modern practice of education. Take 'prudence', for example. In Aquinas' scheme, this is not so much to do with being cautious in reaching judgements, but more with working hard to identify the right means to particular ends in specific circumstances. However, before anyone imagines that here we have an ancient theological endorsement of teaching by objectives, Aquinas makes clear that 'prudence' is centrally about *ethical* deliberation – that is, about thinking through and taking counsel about what *ought* to be done to achieve one's purposes. Thus 'prudence', while it is most assuredly about the business of choosing ends, is chiefly about identifying through reflection the most morally justifiable means to achieving them. Its status as a 'cardinal' virtue then lies in the fact that it instructs us to find those means which can be defended ethically.

'Fortitude' is relevant at this point. According to Aquinas, it teaches us the importance of not being distracted from pursuing our proper and noble ends by the attraction of immediate pleasures or short-term advantage. Translated into the education context, 'fortitude' offers a warning about the consequences of pursuing 'quick-fix' policies that appear to fit well with an immediate problem, but which may have no enduring merit. It also impresses on teachers the importance of persevering professionally in situations that might to any other person seem impossible or extremely difficult – of showing courage in adversity, in other words, particularly when this involves motivating and teaching 'difficult' pupils about whom it is tempting to have low expectations.

'Justice', of course, leavens the whole process. While 'temperance' orders us in ourselves, the cardinal virtue of 'justice' requires those who follow it to consider the common good of society. Specifically, for Aquinas, it is about rendering what is due or owed to another. As such, it invites educators to think of the wider implications of the decisions they reach and pursue in the course of their work. For school managers, in particular, it may constrain them to take more into account the needs of other schools alongside the ones they lead. This has particular relevance in settings where competition between schools is being exacerbated by local market conditions that disable the capacity of some of them to succeed.

Aquinas' cardinal virtues are human virtues. 'Faith', 'hope' and 'charity', on the other hand, are 'supernatural' ones insofar as they raise our minds to things that are above nature. 'Hope' is a special case here. In Aquinas' writings its object is twofold: first, the future good that one desires and, second, the help by which one expects to attain it. As one would expect, God is the object of hope in Aquinas' philosophy. Moreover, because hope is ultimately only realizable through divine means, it requires a modicum of humility on the part of those who practise it. As Aquinas remarks, 'hope goes wrong and is mistaken when you rely on your own strengths'.

Hope, mutuality and experimentation

Aspects of Aquinas' theistic interpretations of hope are capable of secular, including educational, interpretation, in the sense that hopefulness, as experienced by those who have it, entails both anticipating future happiness and *trusting in present help to come to it*. This is something any good teacher would quickly be able to identify with, in the sense that being such a person entails having both high expectations of students' potential as well as faith that the educational process will realize them.

The philosopher Immanuel Kant appeared to recognize this as well, remarking in his magnum opus, *The Critique of Pure Reason*, first published in 1781, that 'all the interests of [his] reason, speculative as well as practical, combine in the following three questions: What can I know? What ought I to do? And for what may I hope?' (1978, para. 805). Kant emphasizes what is at stake in this last question by claiming, in terms reminiscent of Aquinas' earlier, that 'all hoping is directed to happiness'. However, having declared that the concept of hope is central both to his thinking and living happily, Kant nowhere explicitly develops a full-blown analysis of its character. Some of his twentieth-century successors, on the other hand, have given it a fuller treatment, and in roughly similar ways.

For example, central to the thesis developed by Martin Heidegger in his monumental study *Being and Time* (1962) is the proposition that human existence is temporality. The *is* here is fundamental. For Heidegger is not suggesting that human beings simply exist in time; rather that being human entails, in terms reminiscent of the kind of craft knowledge good teachers are said to possess, the capacity simultaneously to be at once ahead, behind and alongside oneself. In fact, in Heidegger's schema, 'Being' is literally 'ecstatic' – or, as he graphically puts it, a form of 'self-projective throwness' in the course of which past, present and future are articulated.

Thus conceived, hope is interpreted not so much as a matter of positively 'looking forward' – though that is a significant part of it – but *a way of living prospectively in and engaging purposefully with the past and present*. Gabriel Marcel says much the same, defining hope as the 'memory of the future' (1951, p. 53) which Ludema and his colleagues translate as the process whereby people 'make a kind of triangulation between the past, present and future, which frees them from the limits of momentary time and space and allows them to make certain global judgements about life and existence' (1997, p. 1039). Something very similar may be said about the process of education to the degree that it entails working positively with what is initially given in order to realize something that is immanent and wished for. There is a clear sense too in which teaching itself is an activity both within and without time, undertaken in one place, but not delimited by it.

The state of being hopeful, however, is not a passive or empty one. On the contrary, it implicitly involves adopting a critical reflective attitude towards prevailing circumstances. Indeed, hope often creates discontent, inasmuch as a person's hopes for the future may make them very dissatisfied with things as they are presently, especially if they get in the way of making progress. Consequently, discontent of this kind often draws attention to a significant absence or gap in how certain matters are currently experienced, allied to a wish to change them for the better. Ludema and his colleagues make the same point, stressing the way in which hoping is a 'continuous movement toward the superlative, the sublime' (1977, p. 1037). Much the same, of course, may be said of the proper practice of education which is premised upon the hope that teaching and learning will lead to improvement, a form of the sublime, even. This premise explains the frustrations that frequently occasion classroom teaching that all too often entail working against the grain of conditions that are antithetical to effective learning.

To say that someone is hopeful is thus to refer to a disposition they possess which results in them being positive about experience or particular aspects of that experience. Being hopeful also involves the belief that something good, which does not presently apply to one's own life, or the life of others, could still materialize, and so it is yearned for as a result. Being hopeful consequently encourages outgoingness as well as a fundamental openness towards one's environment, including, crucially, the people in it. This last element of the equation cannot be stressed enough. For hope, as Ludema (2000) reminds us, is 'fundamentally a relational construct', rather than an emotional or a cognitive possession of individuals. Lionel Tiger argues in similar vein, stating that hope is an 'essential vitamin for social processes. If everybody awoke each day to announce "It's hopeless", there would soon be no plausible tomorrow and no continuous social arrangements' (1999,

p. 622). Marcel concurs, arguing that hope 'is only possible at the level of the *us* . . . and does not exist on the level of the solitary ego' (1951, p. 10). In fact, Marcel inscribes the *us* here with a form of love (specifically, *agape*, which literally means 'self-giving love'), a theme to which I will return towards the end of this chapter where I commend a particular way of bringing the hope back into the practice of teaching in those contexts where it is otherwise difficult to feel anything but pessimism.

Mutuality is then both a source for and a potential outcome of hope, the latter of which is closely bound up with the willingness to experiment, to make choices, to be adventurous. Accordingly, hope has a creative role in encouraging the development of imaginative solutions to seemingly intractable difficulties. To that extent, hope 'is in love with success rather than failure' (Bloch, 1986, p. 1). Specifically, it can visualize a state of affairs not yet existing and, more than this, can both anticipate as well as prepare the ground for something new. Jürgen Moltmann makes this same point, observing that 'unless hope has been aroused and is alive, there can be no planning' (1971, p. 178). The resonance here with the education project hardly requires elaboration, other than to remark that the wish to succeed as a teacher is likely to be accompanied by a yearning hope to do well, allied to a propensity to innovate in order to achieve one's ends.

Absolute and ultimate hope

Godfrey's (1987) own analysis of hope helps us to make further sense of what I have said about it so far. Like me, he draws on Marcel's 'metaphysics of hope' (1951, 1962, 1965), distinguishing two kinds of hope: *absolute* hope and *ultimate* hope. Absolute hope connects with a particular kind of positive orientation to the world – one that entails an openness or readiness of spirit towards the future. According to Godfrey, a person who has absolute hope is someone who, in hoping, sets no condition or limits – is not ready ultimately to despair in the face of disappointment.

While hope needs despair as its opposite (Marcel, 1965, p. 82), despair itself is the enemy of progress because it lacks a faith in the future. Indeed, despair frequently leads to a form of abject pessimism resulting in the grudging acceptance of the status quo (Nesse, 1999). As a result, despair almost always compromises radically people's capacity to act to improve things on behalf of others. Centrally, it can also undermine confidence generally. Looked at from this perspective, absolute hope may be thought of as a vital coping resource in the struggle against despair. Certainly, it can help to galvanize and re-double all our efforts, and not only those of teachers, to overcome nega-tive circumstances that otherwise appear to be beyond reparation. As Marcel says, 'hope is a spring; it is the leaping of a gulf' (1965, p. 86).

Absolute hope entails a basic, even naïve, kind of faith in the future and of the prospects for reform and renewal. This is what Jonathan Sacks, Britain's Chief Rabbi, seems to be inferring in his remark that being hopeful is about 'retaining our sense of the underlying goodness of the world' (1997, p. 267). Christopher Lasch, echoing this senti-ment, states that hope of this kind implies 'a deep-seated trust in life that appears absurd to those who lack it' (1991, p. 81). Marcel con-curs, remarking that 'to hope is to put one's faith in reality, to assert that it contains the means of triumphing over all dangers' (1965, p. 82). Thus understood, it is, in Vaclav Havel's words, 'an orientation of the spirit, an orientation of the heart. . . . It is not the conviction that something will [by definition] turn out well, but the certainty that some-thing makes sense, regardless of how it turns out' (1990, p. 181). For Havel, hope is a 'dimension of the soul . . . [that] . . . transcends the world that is immediately experienced' (ibid.). Similarly, Marcel sees it as 'the prolongation into the unknown of an activity which is central – that is to say, rooted in being' (1962, p. 33).

Although Havel and Marcel are not speaking specifically about the experience of being a teacher, their sentiments connect with it none the less. For most teachers are able to appreciate the unpredictable nature of their work, while at the same time acknowledging that, when it is undertaken seriously, it adds up to more than appearances might otherwise suggest. Although few teachers would probably say as much, many would be able to identify with the suggestion that the educational process always transcends what can be directly observed in it to the degree that it adds up to far more than the sum of its parts. This aspect of teaching is probably what people are referring to when they call it an 'art', which is partly why, I suppose, when it 'works' it can both inspire and uplift all concerned. Confidence of course is crucial to the process. But being hopefully confident does not mean that teachers are therefore excused from ever being sceptical of their abilities. On the contrary, the very ambiguity of the teacher–learner transaction can have the effect of fostering serious self-doubt among those more sensitive practitioners who have particularly reflec-tive approaches towards their work.

While ultimate hope complements its absolute variant, it differs from it in being an *aimed* hope; that is to say, unlike absolute hope it has an object or, more accurately, a better specific state of affairs in mind.

As Godfrey remarks, 'its simple objectives [may be] one's own benefit, another's benefit, or a shared life' (1987, p. 152). Either way, ultimate hope refracts back on the present, holding up to it the prospect of a better way of life – for oneself, for others and for society generally – while recognizing that there are likely to be obstacles on the way that will need to be challenged and overcome. Walter Benjamin's idea of 'Messianic time', which he tantalizingly and briefly outlines in his essay 'Thesis on the philosophy of history', reinforces some of these themes. Benjamin writes of the importance of 'establishing a conception of the future as the "time of the now" which is shot through with chips of Messianic time' (1973, p. 266) – in other words, anticipations *in the here and now* of a better future.

More recently, another Benjamin has integrated these analyses into a compelling and fascinating exploration of how we may think philosophically about the present through the leitmotiv of hope. Andrew Benjamin's *Present Hope* (1997) concludes that hope is best understood as a vital part of living to the full in the present – a form of *realized* eschatology without which it is not possible to engage either meaningfully or authentically with one's immediate life or the contemporary world. These religious emphases – which in Andrew Benjamin's case are inflected by a personal commitment to Judaism – are also manifest in Jürgen Moltmann's highly influential *Theology of Hope* (1967) which seeks to show how Protestant Christian theology can set out from hope and begin to consider its themes in an eschatological light. A similar approach, informed interestingly by Heideggerian categories, is found in John Macquarrie's *Principles of Christian Theology* which concludes that 'hope belongs to the eschatological dimension of the Christian life and, from the ethical point of view, provides a dynamic for action' for *where we are now* (1966, p. 451).

Enemies of hope 1: Cynicism

Both ultimate and absolute hope articulate awkwardly with modern-day cynicism. A cynic today is not the same person the Ancient Greeks meant by the term. For them the cynic was a critic of contemporary culture on the basis of reason and natural law – a revolutionary rationalist, a follower of Socrates. My impression is that many contemporary cynics seem unwilling to follow anybody in particular and appear to have no obvious criterion of truth or set of fixed values, other than to be cryptically critical of most things.

Of course, there is a role for this, inasmuch as some cynics can draw pessimistic attention in ironic, sometimes humorous, ways to the shortcomings of what for the rest of us are assumed features of the world. Relatedly, being a 'pessimist of the intellect' (Gramsci, 1992, p. 12) – that is to say, someone who subjects all significant knowledge claims to critical scrutiny – may be a necessary condition for arguing against conceptions of the future that are dangerously ambitious or narrowly conservative and reactionary. However, overbearing and persistent cynical expressions of pessimism may undermine hopefulness. The sociologist Anthony Giddens has it about right, I think, when he observes that cynical pessimism 'is not a formula for action, and in an extreme form . . . leads only to paralyzing depression' (1990, p. 137), which I suspect is why Marcel saw 'death at its heart' (1962, p. 43). Peter Sloterdijk's (1987) exposition of the cynical mind-set agrees, concluding that it represents a form of melancholic enlightened false-consciousness.

There is a sense too in which cynicism of this sort starts out in any event from the wrong premise. Cynics are fond of telling hopeful people how silly they are to hold on to their aspirations in the face of apparently overwhelming contrary evidence. What they fail to recognize is that out of such hopefulness grows surprising novelty and success. After all, as the philosopher A.C. Grayling (2001) reminds us, 'most of what has moved the world onwards began as hope; all of what has moved it backwards has involved its death'. Cynics might still argue that, because so much hope realizes very little or nothing by way of results, this makes it a form of mere wishful thinking. But this, as Grayling tells us, 'is to see things upside down. For the value of hope [certainly of absolute hope] is independent of its realizations – it is in significant part an end in itself, allied [after Aquinas' cardinal virtues] to courage, persistence and imagination.' Consequently, the state of being hopeful can reveal much about a person's character. Grayling puts this point very well, observing that 'you discover more about people when you learn about their hopes than when you count their achievements, for the best of what we are lies in what we hope to be'.

This does not mean of course that either absolute or ultimate hope always triumph or even – and here I am conscious of a profound paradox – that either requires optimism for it to enable us to cope better with adversity. For, while both hope and optimism stand opposed to pessimism, they also differ from one another. Well, not exactly. It is probably more accurate to say that this claim applies more thoroughly to the relationship optimism has with ultimate rather than absolute hope. Optimism, somewhat akin to absolute hope, is a mood that often misses the ambiguity of the world, with the result that it fails sometimes to consider seriously its negative features. As a result it can translate quickly into brash, complacent, even insensitive forms of behaviour. By contrast, ultimate hope, because it is an aimed hope, lives in the awareness of the world's limitations and remains vulnerable to evidence that counts against it. Understood along these lines, ultimate hope lapses into false optimism only when its intellectual side abdicates responsibility for criticizing the objects it proposes.

Looking at all of this from another angle, there is nothing clearly odd in my remarking that, while I am not overly optimistic of a quick resolution to a current difficulty, I remain none the less hopeful that in the long run something will turn up. Indeed, being hopeful in such situations, as I implied above, is often fundamentally about seeking a positive outcome because it is right to do so, irrespective of the constraints of the current situation that make its achievement in the short term highly unlikely. However, having said that, it is also important not to persist, either in the short or long term, in the hopeful pursuit of something that is clearly a lost cause. To do so is a waste of both time and energy, each of which could be more usefully deployed in pursuing more constructive and potentially realizable projects.

Much the same may be said of those who seek out soft rather than challenging solutions to problems. As Sophocles is reported to have once said: 'I have nothing but scorn for the mortal who comforts himself with hollow hopes.' Gerald Grace's distinction between 'complex' and 'simple hope' is relevant at this point, notably for the way in which it draws into the equation the importance of grounding one's aspirations for the future in a comprehensive analysis of those factors which structurally inhibit reform along particular lines. In pleading caution in this way, Grace is not for one second encouraging conservatism, but rather an intelligent as opposed to evangelistic engagement with the possibilities of change (1994, pp. 48 and 57).

Enemies of hope 2: Fatalism

While optimism is not a necessary condition for being hopeful, fatalism undoubtedly works against its emergence and consequences. Because it implies a total, or near total, determination of events, fatalism can have the most destructive and corrosive of effects, particularly in the education context, which relies so much on hopefulness to be able to do its best work. Fatalism is also profoundly conservative. In Theodore Adorno's words, 'it offers the advantage of veiling all deeper-lying causes of distress and thus promoting acceptance of the given. Moreover, by strengthening the sense of fatality, dependence and obedience, it paralyses the will to change objective conditions in any respect' (1974, quoted in Grint and Hogan, 1993, p. 1).

Despite these negative aspects, fatalism is not unheard of in the school staffroom. Usually, it takes the form of a way of speaking that entails teachers cynically rationalizing existing or proposed practices and current predicaments that for others appear neither inevitable nor unavoidable. 'What can you do?'; 'It's just the way things are'; 'It didn't work then, so why should it work now?' are just a few of the ways fatalism of this sort finds oral expression. Such talk can have very negative consequences if inflected along deficit lines, such as in the case of assuming that children from particular kinds of social backgrounds, usually working class, are, by definition, less likely to do as well at school as their middle-class counterparts. Much the same danger rears its head in statements which take for granted that schools serving areas of cumulative social and economic disadvantage are always going to fail to provide a quality education. Such fatalistic expectations are the scourge of an education programme premised on hopefulness.

Fate's ineluctability has consequences not only for how teachers react to the prospects of change, but also for how they relate to the prevailing distributions of authority and hierarchies of power in the schools within which they work, that may themselves be in need of reform if new windows of opportunity are to be opened. The authoritarian male school manager who seeks to subordinate his staff's interests to his own is able to induce quiescence partially through making his exercise of power, and the culture of control to which it gives rise, appear part of the inevitable order of things. Applications of absolute hope, on the other hand, can render such a view problematic, to the extent that its openness of spirit offers up a challenge to the maintenance of the taken for granted.

Enemies of hope 3: Relativism

While fatalism places impossible limits on what can be hoped for, relativism, particularly of the postmodern kind, avoids commitment of any kind and leaves its followers in a quandary about what it is reasonable to look forward to. The central intellectual tenets of the postmodern attitude are the problem here. These entail a three-fold set of rejections (see Flax, 1990, pp. 32–4): a rejection, first, of all essentialist and transcendental conceptions of human nature; a rejection, second, of unity, homogeneity, totality, closure and identity; and, third, a rejection of the possibility of establishing truth and certainty.

In their place, we are offered contingency, fragmentation, particularity and difference.

In many ways this intellectual agenda is liberating, even democratizing, in its refusal to acknowledge the dictates of hierarchy and universalism. Certainly, in cultural terms, it has allowed outmoded canons of taste and conservatism to be challenged and abolished. On the other hand, as Kate Soper argues (1993), it has also led to a radical relativizing of concepts such as worth in the field of aesthetics, freedom in ethics, and truth and objectivity in epistemology. Also, in the fields of education and politics, if taken to its logical conclusion, postmodernism removes completely any basis for the development of principled positions that might inform action.

However, on the plus side, postmodernism does urge upon us the need to recognize that there is probably no one type of society or education that will serve as an ideal for all people. People are diverse – infinitely so, perhaps, but in any case indefinitely so. They have widely differing preferences and aspirations; their lifestyles may be utterly different as well and they may have diverse views of the kind of world they wish to inhabit and the sort of education it should provide. It is for this reason that the philosopher Robert Nozick provocatively offers a list of thirty-odd diverse people and asks rhetorically whether there is really one kind of life that is best for each of them (1974, p. 310). It perhaps makes the point with sufficient strength to note that three of the names on his list are another philosopher, Ludwig Wittgenstein, the actress, Elizabeth Taylor, and the comedian, Lenny Bruce. It is surely incredible, writes Nozick, to think that they could be made to agree, with little note of dissent, on particular matters of social policy, leading him to conclude that there cannot be a single vision of the perfect life, least of all one that is imposed on everyone, but rather a multiplicity of aspirations from which people can choose voluntarily the one that best fits their circumstances.

Nozick is surely right to warn us against seizing on one particular vision and forcing its pattern on society as a whole. Indeed, the history of how socialist ideals have been translated into blueprints for communism – entailing more often than not the suppression of individual freedom linked to modes of dictatorial governance – provides a sufficient reminder of the folly of such an approach. However, equally, Nozick's warning should not be used as an excuse for claiming that 'anything goes' and avoiding as a result all principled positions. That in fact is not a conclusion to be drawn from his analysis, which proceeds by insisting on the importance of seeking out common normative standards by which people from diverse backgrounds may come to terms with different ways of life.

The search for common normative strands is likely to be embarked upon successfully only in contexts where people feel free to argue about and seek to persuade others of the merits of their value positions and the ways of life upon which they are based and to which they give rise. Thus, rather than surrender to the kind of nihilism evident in some extreme forms of postmodernism, we should instead seek to realize communities in which there is the possibility of the development of a vocabulary of values in which all can share. For, while postmodernism is correct to tell us that there is no final proof, no final end, of what is right and wrong, this does not preclude the need for continuing debate about what each might mean.

Enemies of hope 4: Fundamentalism and traditionalism

While relativism leaves us all at sea about what to hope for, fundamentalism entails an evangelical-like adherence to tradition, which places limits on what can be looked forward to.

In setting out one's hopes for the future, there is however nothing contradictory in appealing to a tradition or set of traditions. On the contrary, being hopeful and utopian, as will become apparent, sometimes entails a form of nostalgia or future-oriented remembering, in the course of which a vision of a good society is defined as much in terms derived from recollections and reconstructions of times past as from fantastic notions of future states of affairs. My concern is that this process may lead to an unnecessary narrowing of options or, as in the case of fundamentalism, to an irrational commitment to just one course or collection of courses of action. Indeed, some forms of nostalgia or tradition adherence can quickly become either an excuse for, or a precursor of, fatalism. Much, of course, hinges on what is meant by tradition, traditionalism and fundamentalism in this context.

There are obvious difficulties of interpretation here. 'Tradition', for a start, is a notoriously difficult term to pin down. This does not stop it cropping up all the time in discussions of the future direction of education policy. There are, for example, any number of polemical accounts to hand suggesting that schools should reflect 'traditional' values, including pedagogical ones. It was not so long ago, for instance, that both Britain's former Prime Minister, John Major, and a member of its Royal family, Prince Charles, were telling us about the obvious benefits of 'chalk and talk' teaching methods (see Chitty and Simon, 1993, p. 144; MacLeod, 1996).

Much the same applies to the version of tradition that has found its way into the present British government's education policy discourse. Thus Stephen Byers, one of its former schools ministers, once commented that New Labour's 'third way' approach to school reform meant 'applying traditional values to a changed setting' (Byers, 1998). The question of which traditional values need to be reapplied – and, indeed, to what 'changed setting' – was left mostly unasked at the time. But then, that is what an appeal to tradition frequently entails: the celebration of a particular way of doing something, the merits of which are assumed to be greater than any alternative.

Traditions, in the education context and elsewhere, are therefore capable of being either inclusive and exclusive. In the latter case, this can have frustrating consequences for the educational visionary bent on applying a dose of ultimate hope to the process of school reform. Wilf Carr and Anthony Hartnett spell out the double-edged implications of this very well:

> Educational traditions contain ideas about what constitutes real education and real schools and they guide people's instincts about what can and should be done . . . They provide languages, vocabularies and political repertoires which both make possible new ways of thinking and act as boundaries beyond which it is dangerous to go.
>
> (1996, p. 107)

Traditions thus defined are constituted by sets of ideas, rituals and repertoires about what can and should be done. In Eric Hobsbawm's words, they also 'seek to inculcate certain values and norms' and, in so doing, 'attempt to establish continuity with a suitable historic past' (1983, p. 1). There is no suggestion being made here that this is a bad thing. After all, we need traditions to help us to make sense of our experience and guide our actions. What is at stake here is not to do with the need for tradition – which is assumed – but rather with the manner in which traditions are drawn upon and the consequences of this process for what can be hoped for.

Some applications of tradition, as in the case of being fatalistic, can seriously delimit optimism's room for manoeuvre. Because tradition, more or less, always offers a historical and cultural ratification of a contemporary order (Williams, 1977, p. 115f.), it plays a crucial role in *justifying and legitimating* particular courses of action, policies and sets of practices. Accordingly, in certain circumstances, an appeal to a particular tradition can serve as a source of support for the exercise of power over others and for securing obedience to commands. Thus, the reciting of certain patriotic traditions, such as those that stress nationhood and heritage, facilitate the mobilization for governments of measures that privilege the 'national interest' – not just economically, but also militarily, as in the case of war or threats of war.

Equally, certain 'domestic' traditions are appealed to by particular kinds of men to justify the continued subjugation of women, both in the home and in the workplace generally. Tradition is also used by some adults to compel young people, including their own children, to do what they are told simply by virtue of the authority they assume to be vested in their status as an older person who 'traditionally' is expected to be 'looked up to'. Some teachers, too, draw on this tradition, or a variant of it, when imposing their will on their students, particularly when they misbehave or 'answer back'. These specific invocations of tradition, which are often used to exert power or to reinforce relations of power ('I am doing this and you must respond thus because it is traditional – and therefore proper – to do so'), is what I understand by tradition*alism*: that is to say, a reified appeal to the notion of tradition itself to support beliefs or actions that might at other times or through alternative eyes be deemed unacceptable (Giddens, 1994, p. 85).

At such times, the rhetorical defence of a particular tradition may give rise to a form of fundamentalism in which its truth is insisted upon and the requirement to cite reasons for believing it is denied. In education, the division of school knowledge into subjects, the need for school uniform and the value of rote-learning and memorization are often defended by 'traditionalists' in precisely this way. In the first case, the epistemological arbitrariness of some subject boundaries is rarely acknowledged; in the second, no reference is made to the relatively short history of strict dress codes for pupils attending publicly funded schools or their cultural specificity; in the third, there is a neglect of the medieval historic context within which 'learning by heart' was first appropriated as the most expedient way of remembering and communicating important 'truths' in the absence of mass publication of sacred and other texts.

Despite their continued influence on how schooling is practised, all forms of fundamentalism connect awkwardly with those aims of education which stress growth in learners' understanding. Understood as the unthinking application of tradition to questions about how best to proceed, it is also a problem for the thoroughgoing utopian concerned to explore the value of alternative ways of proceeding – particularly ways that imply a critique of traditional, or taken-for-granted, ways of acting. So, while I have no doubt that traditions will continue to flourish in the educational context, indeed are likely to be invented within it, my argument is that it would be better if they did so on the basis of argument and evidence instead of appeals to their alleged internal authority and integrity. My starting point in all of this is again Giddens, who correctly remarks that 'tradition (today) must more and more be contemplated, defended, sifted through, in relation to the awareness that there exists a variety of other ways of doing things' (1994, p. 83).

Hope and the virtues of teaching

Both ultimate and absolute hope, as we learned earlier from Aquinas' teaching about fortitude, are attitudes that buffer people against falling into apathy in the face of tough going, which arguably is why educators cannot responsibly abdicate either in their work in schools or elsewhere. They must not only take them seriously and seek to embody them in their actions; they need also to find ways of fostering each among their students and colleagues, and especially now given that so much in our world, privately, nationally and globally, is characterized by chronic uncertainty. I would go further and assert that to teach how to live without certainty, and yet without being paralysed by hesitation, is perhaps one of the chief things a good education offers. Mary Warnock says much the same, stating that of all the attributes she would like to see in her children or pupils, 'the attribute of hope would come high, even top of my list. To lose hope is to lose the capacity to want or desire anything; to lose, in fact, the wish to live' (1986, p. 182). Indeed, to lack hope is to lack a vital spiritual energy and to run the danger of lapsing into lethargy and indifference.

No small wonder, then, that students with high ultimate hope are more motivated and committed to their studies than their counterparts with a more pessimistic disposition (Goleman, 1996, pp. 86f.). The same, it seems, is the case with teachers. For, as Collinson and her colleagues reveal in their small-scale comparative empirical study of teacher motivation, exemplary teachers who have ultimate hope and who can demonstrate it in the classroom are able to motivate even the most disaffected of students. Their analysis demonstrates well the manner in which the teachers they investigated 'look for strengths in their students and for a way of helping each one as an individual, to take them from where they are at, as a starting point, and progress from there' (1999, p. 4). The teachers studied also focus on 'the possibility and worth of what is hoped for' – that is, they help their students to learn and experience success. This success, however, is not interpreted in exclusively academic terms, but rather in its broadest educational sense, including the fostering of a positive attitude towards learning for life.

In addition, the exemplary teachers in this study desire simultaneously that they should also do well *as teachers*. In other words, 'for these teachers, holding high expectations applies to themselves as well as to the students' (ibid., p. 7). In ways that again connect with Aquinas' cardinal virtues, tenacity and patience it seems are central features of this professional outlook. For, time and again, these teachers draw attention to their unwillingness to give up in the face of difficulty and, indeed, to model their persistence in this respect so as to encourage a similar attitude among the students whom they teach. The approach these teachers adopt to their work suggests too that hope can be mediated – perhaps even taught – within the educational context via the adoption of cultures of learning that accentuate the positive rather than the negative, most notably through praising effort instead of focusing on lack of success.

Padraig Hogan, in terms also reminiscent of Aquinas', suggests much the same. Occupying a pivotal position in the list he draws up of the virtues of teaching are 'circumspect honesty, patience and persistence, frankness, originality, a judicious faith in pupils . . . and a categorical sense of care for [them]' (1996, p. 14). In creating this list, Hogan reaffirms a moral role for the teacher as a significant and influential adult figure dedicated to the business of helping pupils to realize their full potential through acquiring a hopeful disposition towards both their studies and their lives generally. Although he does not say as much, I would go further and argue that, because education is essentially a future-oriented project concerned to bring about improvement, specifically *growth* in the learner's knowledge and understanding, successful teaching requires its practitioners to teach with hope in mind.

Of course, teaching, as the author of the article that began this chapter illustrates, does not always reflect such a grand purpose, nor turn out well when it does. On the contrary, as Daniel Liston also tellingly says, 'in many a teacher's heart there is [today] an enveloping darkness. It is a darkness that may not be as penetrating and pervasive as clinical depression . . . but nevertheless amounts to a devastating sense that the education, teaching and life we have clung to with such hope and promise are losing their grip'. Indeed, for many teachers, 'the promise of education to transform, ennoble and enable, to create the conditions for new understandings of our worlds and ourselves, have become tired and devalued promissory notes' (Liston, 2000, p. 81).

If this is an accurate assessment of what the experience of being a schoolteacher is currently like for a growing number of its practitioners, it raises the question of what can be done to counter the profession's emerging sense of hopelessness and associated low morale. No doubt improved remuneration and better working conditions would help, but these are surely not sufficient.

What may also be needed is an effort of moral will on the part of teachers themselves and their managers, employers and trainers to revitalize that aspect of what it means to be a teacher that connects with the virtues of teaching identified by Hogan above. Drawing on Murdoch's (1970) Platonic interpretation of 'God' and 'Good', Liston writes relatedly of the need for some teachers to recapture 'the love of teaching . . . [which enables its exponents] to venture [once more] into that space where hope and possibility exist' (Liston, 2000, p. 94). The use of the word 'love' in this context is central to Liston's vision, as it is of course to St Paul's trilogy of theological virtues which articulates faith and hope with love. It also resonates with Marcel's existentialism which, as we learned earlier, sees hope as 'a protestation inspired by love' (1965, p. 87).

Liston uses Murdoch's thesis to brilliant effect, arguing that what is currently needed is a re-moralizing of teaching that 'places an understanding of the "Good" and an orientation to love at [its] very centre' (ibid.). This call to a 'larger love' is an appeal to teachers, and all those concerned with schooling, to recover 'the idea of 'Good' as a focal point of [professional] reflection' (Murdoch, 1970, p. 69): such a 'larger teaching love . . . attends [fully] to the situation, to the students in their classes, in an attempt to see things more clearly, to find ways to connect students with the grace of things. . . . It looks for the Good in students and those teaching settings; it attempts to see students in ways that assume and build up the Good' (Liston, 2000, p. 97).

A crucial aspect of this project ought to entail an effort on the part of individual teachers to connect such a 'larger love of teaching' with the pursuit of what the Catholic Bishops of England and Wales (Catholic Education Service) define as the 'common good in education', which they identify closely with 'promoting the dignity of the human person' through policies for schools that 'encourage and help students of *all* abilities to improve the quality of their work' as well as a respect for difference and value diversity (1997, p. 8)

But this 'larger love of teaching', and the pursuit of the 'common good in education', is unlikely to be revived within a context – such as the one largely prevailing at the moment in British schools – whereby teachers are routinely devalued and their efforts centrally regulated in ways that suggest a lack of trust in their competence and professionalism. Moreover, the education marketplace within which most of them are now compelled to work is arguably antithetical to attempts on their part to pursue educational aims that seek to ensure equitable distributions of resources and outcomes.

In other words, to 'build up the common good', teachers will need to feel that their best work is valued and their higher motivations applauded, and that they are not in competition with their colleagues for resources and students. 'Naming and shaming' schools and tarnishing the whole profession with a negative brush for the faults of a minority not only frustrate this process, but dangerously inhibit it from ever getting started. To that extent, teachers cannot be expected to shoulder the whole burden for restoring their morale – employers, managers and government each have a role to play; and in playing it, the performance must be sincere, rather than grounded in a form of 'contrived emotionality' (Hartley, 1999) whose apparent empowering aspects are really a mask for further bureaucratic management and autocratic control.

But even this is unlikely to satisfy those pessimists that hold on resolutely to the belief that teaching is by definition an exercise in futility which is incapable of being restored to the dignity I am suggesting it warrants. On the other hand, such individuals, it seems to me, are not just being fatalistic; they are also working against the grain of the educational process. For notwithstanding the many factors that can sometimes make it difficult, even seemingly impossible, to teach effectively some students, every good teacher knows there is built into this transaction the *possibility* that it will realize something for the better. Moreover, it is this tacit knowledge that spurs on to success the exemplary teachers reported on above who clearly take their work and role as public educators seriously.

To be sure, going through the motions with pupils is always an option for any teacher, but it is a course of action that has nothing to do with wanting to educate them, least of all with wanting to help them develop a positive conception of themselves and of the future. As Warnock (1986, p. 183) inspiringly reminds us,

> education is particularly fitted to [encourage hope] . . . To feel competent, able to act, able to change or control things, or even to

create them, these are all aspects of feeling hope . . . To find that today you can begin to do something you could not do yesterday is to begin to hope. For someone to wake up in the morning, thinking 'Good, I can go on with it' whatever 'it' is, this . . . must be the chief goal of education.

In fact, there is a sense in which the identification of any *educational aim* implies an element of absolute hopefulness, though, significantly, given what I wrote earlier, its realization entails working out how best to achieve it incrementally in the present, usually lesson by lesson, and (after Aquinas) in a state of humility coupled with courage and conviction.

Summary

This chapter has outlined a general theory of hope and discussed its implications for the practice of education. This analysis realized three key ideas: that teaching is premised on hope – that is, on the possibility that it will realize improvement of one kind or another; that being hopeful as a teacher facilitates innovation and an earnestness to do well in one's work; and that hope is a relational construct which in the education context requires teachers to look for and build up the 'Good' in their students.

This chapter also took to task four 'enemies' of hope in the educational context and generally: cynicism, fatalism, relativism and fundamentalism. It challenged cynicism's false consciousness; objected to fatalism's conservatism; rebutted relativism's lack of moral and political will; and criticized fundamentalism's blinkered adherence to tradition which was seen as a barrier to thinking differently and progressively about the future. The chapter concluded with an appeal to teachers to re-moralize their work by combining hope about it with a larger love of teaching itself.

Chapter 2 will add to this analysis by exploring the way in which applications of the utopian imagination can provide distinctive vocabularies of hope that assist in the creation of new images of positive relational possibility, in turn expanding the range of resources available for the reform and renewal of education.

2 · Utopianism as a vocabulary of hope

> By scanning the field of the possible in which the seal occupies merely a tiny plot, utopias pave the way for a critical attitude and a critical activity.
>
> (Zygmunt Bauman)

Cultural pessimism

During the last two decades of the previous century there took place in the West an enormous growth in negative representations of the possibilities of social, economic and political reform. Drawing on studies from within a very broad range of fields, including ecology, human rights, military history, international relations, criminology, history of science, cultural criticism and political economy, Oliver Bennett (2001) charts this development, identifying four key contemporary 'narratives of decline', relating respectively to the environment, morality, intellectual life and political culture.

In Bennett's overview, cultural pessimism about the environment is centred on negative assessments of the cumulative direct effects of pollution on human health and wildlife and its indirect consequences through impacts on the ozone layer and global warming. Narratives of moral pessimism, on the other hand, focus on the degenerative effects of the morality of nuclear and post-nuclear warfare, the high incidence of torture, genocide and political murder in different parts of the world and the radical increase in criminal activity throughout the Western world over the past forty years. Meanwhile, narratives of intellectual decline point up the limitations of the scientific outlook and the associated demise of the religious one; they also draw attention to the exhausted state of the world of art and the 'dumbing down' of intellectual life in general. The decline of the political sphere, finally, is associated with the negative effects wrought by a globalized capitalist economic order that presently seems to serve its own selfish ends in ways that are largely independent of either political influence˙ or control.

Narratives of decline, as was indicated in my earlier discussion of fatalism, are also evident within education. The forms these take are many and varied. They range from assertions that standards of schooling, teaching, student-learning and pupil behaviour are not as good as they once were, to claims that teaching as a profession is itself under threat because of the alleged de-skilling of teachers' work which critics argue has become over-bureaucratized and too heavily tied to market-driven conceptions of efficiency and effectiveness.

I am less concerned at this point with the truth that may or may not lie behind any of these narratives of decline, as with their effects and consequences. Bennett suggests, correctly I think, that they contribute to a 'generalised negative certainty', entailing a shift in people's thinking that 'produces an endless cycle of automatic negative thoughts, resulting in an incapacity to see the self, the world or the future in anything other than negative terms' (2001, p. 181).

The use here by Bennett of the word 'cycle' is important, inasmuch as it draws attention to the manner in which negative thinking and negative feeling, followed quickly by negative acting, can become closely entwined, producing 'at their worst, a feedback loop, with negative thoughts generating negative feelings which generate more negative thoughts ad infinitum' (ibid., p. 181f.). Sometimes, Bennett observes, this pessimistic feedback loop is fuelled by *negative over-generalizations* based on 'limited evidence which are then extrapolated out into predictions of the future', or supported by *selective abstractions* in which positive information is routinely screened out and only negative data admitted. It can also entail *dichotomous, 'either-or', thinking* in which only polar opposites are entertained, all things being seen as either all good or all bad, and nothing ever being viewed as a mix of both.

The resonance here with the depressive condition is obvious. It also recalls the essay I quoted at the outset of Chapter 1 in which a teacher describes his work in the most extraordinarily negative terms: the children he teaches (all of them) are 'out of control'; none of them will 'get jobs, because there aren't any' (none at all); his school building is (totally) 'unhealthy and badly designed'; and if he 'could leave teaching, he'd go tomorrow'. There is more than a hint in this account of negative over-generalization, selective abstraction and dichotomous thinking. There is also a conviction that the teacher's work circumstances will not improve that much, but rather get worse.

It is almost as if the teacher concerned needs this narrative of professional decline in order to make sense of and survive what he sees as an impossible situation. His culture of pessimism may also be acting as a kind of defence mechanism or, as Bennett puts it, 'a projection on to the external world of a negativity that would otherwise be directed towards himself' (2001, p. 183). In this connection, it could be noteworthy that the teacher ultimately offers no indication of what he might do to resolve the set of dilemmas he is experiencing in his professional life. Rather, he portrays himself as a victim of events and circumstances, including other people's actions and decisions, chiefly, in the latter case, those of 'government and management', both of which are enjoined to support him better in order to cause his sense of professional loyalty and vocation to return.

If my interpretation is accurate, my guess is that the teacher who wrote that essay was probably ignorant of the way in which he was catastrophizing his circumstances, seeing them as totally beyond his control. Some of the aspects of his work situation, let us be clear, are real enough. Many school buildings are in a poor state of repair; an increasing number of pupils are proving difficult to motivate and control; and Government and school management have in recent times made new, and not always welcome, demands on teachers' work and sense of professionalism. To that degree, his narrative of decline may not be just an aspect of the negative judgement he has reached about what it means to be a teacher today, but also a reflection of a personal structure of feeling that has been significantly affected for the worse by the actual circumstances of his work.

This is not to suggest, however, that these circumstances are as immutable as he implies, or as comprehensibly negative as he makes out. On the contrary. Few situations are all bad, and certainly few in the education context. Even if they were, because they are the creation of the human imagination and the consequence of human decision-making, they must therefore, by definition, be susceptible to human change, notwithstanding the challenges involved, particularly when the circumstances concerned are long-standing ones that have proved extremely resistant to reform. On the other hand, undertaking successfully reforms of this kind is unlikely to be assisted by a mode of cultural pessimism that negatively contaminates and undermines the will of teachers to change themselves and the circumstances within which they work.

What therefore may be needed are some positive illusions that help teachers to keep negative thoughts and feelings at bay, or at least in proportion – what Ludema and his colleagues describe as 'vocabularies of hope', which in their schema serve as tools to assist people generally to promote the 'reconstruction of relationships in ways that conform to collective images of the Good' (1997, p. 1021).

Such positive vocabularies, Bennett rightly suggests, can 'act as a bulwark against depression and anxiety, helping to maintain a sense of happiness or contentment. This in turn has been shown to enhance an individual's capacity both to develop rewarding relationships with others and to work productively or creatively' (2001, p. 194). In saying this, Bennett is not for a moment meaning that all forms of pessimism should be condemned. For, as was stressed in Chapter 1, pessimism of the intellect, to take one example, is to be encouraged, not suppressed.

What Bennett endorses rather is a kind of 'depressive realism', in the course of which those who practise it achieve a mentally healthy cognitive articulation of the emotionally optimistic with the intellectually pessimistic. It is the premise of this book that such an articulation is unlikely to be achieved without successfully searching for, locating and internalizing particular vocabularies of hope, of which utopias are significant exemplars.

Utopia and desire

If we ask where and what kind of place is the place of hope, then one answer might be 'utopia'. Although every expression of ultimate hope does not require the exercise of the utopian imagination, all utopias are driven by hope – that is to say, they express the dreams of an age, and they say something about its capacities. Indeed, to the extent that the power of utopian thinking derives from its inherent ability to visualize the future in terms of radically new forms and values, utopianism holds out to optimists of the will the promise of them being able better to reconsider critically their opinions about the most desirable ways in which the economy, society and the state should be organized.

Utopias thus constitute hidden signifiers or projections of people's desires (Harvey, 2000, p. 195; Levitas, 1990, p. 124). They also entail a form of positive escapism into a world uncontaminated by common sense where it is possible simultaneously to imagine and anticipate radical alternatives to the status quo. This description of the utopian impulse anticipates well the chief characteristics of utopias themselves. These frequently include a sense of 'placelessness' and 'timelessness', allied to a 'perfectional emphasis' (Kolnai, 1995), all of which help to redirect our conservative attentions away from the taken for granted towards something new, innovative and progressive (Plattel, 1972).

Journeying to utopia

It is this last feature of the utopian imagination it seems that impressed Michel Foucault, although his writing about the future in *The Order of Things* is heterotopian rather than utopian. In fact, Foucault does not ask us to hope for a particular better form of life as such but, through 'dissolving our myths and sterilising the lyricism of our sentences' (1970, p. xviii), to imagine instead a time so different as to make our own seem arbitrary. The effect is the same, however, for Foucault is encouraging us to suspend our taken-for-granted assumptions about reality in order to envisage it differently.

Louis Marin's (1984) conception of utopia, which is associated with the category of the 'neutral', resonates here as well. He encourages us to understand utopian discourse less as a form of representation, and more as a journey, in the course of which continuous time and ordering loci are suspended, thus allowing reality to be constructed in out-of-the-ordinary ways. Marin's suggestion that the search for utopia may entail some kind of journey is in fact writ large in a lot of utopian texts, many of which begin with a tale of travel to an unknown land, often by sea. This aspect of utopianism possibly explains why Foucault liked so much to use the ship as a metaphor for the creative use of this aspect of his own imagination. 'The sailing vessel' (he once wrote) 'is the heterotopia par excellence. In a civilization without ships the dreams dry up' (1998, p. 185).

It is for this reason alone, I suspect, that applications of the utopian imagination are able sometimes to help dissolve pessimism and introduce a degree of optimism into public discourse (Bailey, 1988). They effect this by the manner in which they illustrate the principle that no matter how bad things appear they can be envisaged differently, and for the better. Indeed, at the core of utopian writing is the triumph of reason over circumstance. Thus, while they do not always provide insight into precisely how things can be made better, utopias usually point up possibilities for change that normally would be either ruled out automatically or never thought about.

Dystopias (or anti-utopias) have the potential to work the same trick, but in the other direction. There is, though, a sense in which utopia and dystopia incorporate each other – the former being about hoping for a transformed future; the latter about anticipating it, while simultaneously fearing the worst! (Kumar, 1991). Terry Eagleton puts this even better, remarking that 'all utopia is . . . at the same time dystopia, since it cannot help reminding us of how we are bound fast by history in the very act of trying to set us free from that bondage' (2000a, p. 31). Richard Coyne comes to the same conclusion: 'The concept of utopia is never far from its converse, the dystopia, and the components of one writer's utopia may constitute the dystopia of another' (1999, p. 21).

Utopian distancing: making the familiar strange

Utopias, it is suggested, must always have content. But it is ultimately their *function* in promoting the consideration of imaginative alternatives that makes them utopian. Zygmunt Bauman, elaborating this suggestion, says that utopias 'relativise the present . . . [by] undermin[ing] the sense that the way things are is inevitable and immutable by presenting alternative versions of society' (1976, p. 13). Barbara Goodwin concurs, arguing that the primary function of utopia is to distance us from immediate circumstances so as to develop an alternative schema that points towards change and the promotion of human happiness (Goodwin and Taylor, 1982, ch. 1 and p. 207). Andre Gorz's positive assessment of utopias is similarly inflected, stating that they 'provide us with the distance from the existing state of affairs which allows us to judge what we are doing in the light of what we could or should do' (1999, p. 113).

These functional analyses of utopia complement Karl Mannheim's (1979) who sees it as one means of helping 'to shatter, either partially or wholly, the order of things prevailing at the time' (p. 173). Similarly, Terry Eagleton argues that 'in a great deal of utopian fiction, alternative worlds are simply devices for embarrassing the world we actually have. The point is not to go elsewhere, but to use elsewhere as a reflection on where you are' (2000a, p. 33).

Thus understood, utopias encourage us to ask and answer the question, 'for *what* may I hope?' As Levitas states, 'they tell us in a way that we cannot directly ascertain where the felt absences are in people's lives – the spaces, that is, that utopia offers to fill, whether in fantasy or reality' (1990a, p. 189). Similarly, in her review of feminist utopias, Lucy Sargisson argues that utopian texts 'break and transform societal and cultural rules. In so doing . . . they create new conceptual spaces in which radically different ways of being can be imagined' (1996, p. 2). They achieve this by encouraging the perception that the social reality of the reader is neither static nor unchangeable. This perception in turn realizes a form of estrangement whereby the commonplace is rendered unusual and unfamiliar, serving to distance the reader from social reality, while at the same time engendering the idea that it could be changed in favour of a better alternative (Hogan, n.d., p. 14). Indeed, because the reader's world, like the imaginary one of the utopian text, is a world constructed, it becomes open to the possibility of change. In Tom Moylan's words, the 'fresh view' created by such juxtaposition holds within it 'the seeds for changing the present society . . . [by] conveying a sense that the world is not fixed once and for all' (1986, p. 35).

Daydreaming to utopia

This interpretation of the function of utopianism links well with Ernst Bloch's (1986) suggestion that utopias should be regarded sometimes as a form of 'anticipatory illumination or pre-appearance' or, on other occasions, as 'daydreams of that which is not yet'. In using such graphic terminology, Bloch is seeking to illustrate the way in which utopianism is not just a human creation, but a key aspect of what it actually means to be human. Utopian daydreaming, he insists, is a significant way in which people reflect on future possibilities and in which, especially, they engage with the vicissitudes of their everyday lives, thus facilitating a degree of psychic equilibrium that helps them to resist over-deterministic interpretations of how they should be lived. We all daydream about our next holiday, the home we would like to live in, the person whom we would prefer to partner, the person we would like to be, and the job we would ideally like to have. Such utopian daydreams sustain life and give some direction and purpose to it, providing effort is put into making them real. In the education context, of course, they enable teachers to anticipate how best to teach particular subject matter; they also foster in their thinking high expectations of what pupils can achieve.

Utopia and nostalgia

'Good' utopias, like daydreams, are always future-oriented and thus contrast with the utopian veneer projected by the conservative image of a desired society in which traditions that assume old hierarchies and seek to preserve antiquated modes of deference and control are given priority. Utopias are about offering radical challenges to the status quo, not reinforcing or reconstructing it. As Eileen Hogan says, 'utopia cannot be "what was" – it is, by definition, progressive' (n.d., p. 28), a view which helps to explain Levitas' claim that utopianism should be considered as 'the necessary starting point for a critical social policy' (2001, p. 463).

This is not to say that the past has nothing to contribute to utopian thinking. On the contrary, certain kinds of nostalgia can contribute a great deal to it. The 'not-yet', or unfulfilled desires of the past, for example, may act as a resource in contemplating an improved immediate present and a better long-term future. As Raymond Williams' discussion (1980, 1983) of 'heuristic utopias' suggests, nostalgia of this sort can assist reflection on the standing of esteemed 'structures of feeling'. Heuristic utopias, he says, are ones that encourage the facility 'to strengthen and confirm existing feelings and relationships which are not at home in the existing order and cannot be lived through in it' (1983, p. 13). Similarly, Boym (2002) writes favourably about a reflective form of nostalgia which is 'critical, self-aware and ethical' rather than a mere pretext for melancholia. David Harvey, echoing these sentiments, considers that particular forms of utopia are capable of 'opening up ways of thinking that have for too long remained foreclosed' (2000, p. 17).

On the other hand, we need to beware of what Louis Marin (1984) cryptically refers to as 'degenerative utopias' – that is to say, forms of spatial play that sanitize and mythologize the limitations of the past so as to make it acceptable in the present. All forms of 'golden ageism' fall into this category, as do the futuristic utopias mirrored in some of the exhibits found in such heterotopia as Disneyland and the former Millennium Dome in Greenwich, London, and in cultural theme parks generally. In each case, we are offered no critique of the past or existing order of things, but rather a comfortable and comforting account of a historical epoch in which its contradictory and dysfunctional features are obscured, or a neutralized assessment of the possibilities and inevitability of technological change.

Utopia and politics

Because they express competing desires for and images of the good society, utopias are inescapably political. Michael Ignatieff puts this more poetically than I ever could, remarking that 'utopian thought is a dream of the redemption of human tragedy through politics' (1994, p. 19). Equally, to the extent that absolute hope transcends the world which is immediately experienced – in Vaclav Havel's words, is 'anchored somewhere beyond its horizons' (1990, p. 181) – its counterpart utopia always 'pushes to the limit' (Walsh, 1993, p. 53), generating political argument as a result rather than obsequious consensus. Consequently, utopian 'elsewheres', as Terry Eagleton reminded us earlier, offer us an important means of taking stock politically of where we are now and of where we may want to go; that is to say, they evoke a future possibility by helping us to escape the constraints of the present.

Objections to utopia

This very positive account of the nature and potential of utopianism, of course, begs a number of major questions. Terry Eagleton, as I mentioned in the Preface, anticipates many of them, drawing attention to the need to make a sharp distinction between 'good' and 'bad' utopias – the former being grounded in practical possibility (what I will later define as 'utopian realism'), the latter in mere wistful thinking.

But even this distinction would not satisfy some of utopia's more ardent critics, who consider utopianism *per se* as constituting a deeply flawed way of thinking. Aurel Kolnai, for example, dismisses it altogether. His critique, however, turns mostly on a philosophically analytical study of the *concept* of utopia which, he argues, is urealizable a priori because it is premised on principles that bracket out the possibility of difference, most notably differences of value. He concludes therefore that utopias have no real content because they do not allow anything to count against them – they are 'out of focus, removed from the perspective in which the concept of perfection alone is meaningful' (1995, pp. 31, 32–3). Similarly, Isaiah Berlin characterizes the utopian imagination as being one that avoids all moral and other forms of deliberation about choice through its adherence to a unitary and static worldview: 'Nothing in utopias alters, for they have reached perfection; there is no need for novelty or change; no one can wish to alter a condition in which all natural human wishes are fulfilled' (1991, p. 20). Other objections to utopianism include its frequent failure to elaborate on a plausible strategy for change; its naive faith in people's capacities to alter things for the better; and its alleged and ill-advised tendency to break radically with the past rather than undertake more piecemeal, incremental reform (see Geus, 1999, ch. 2).

These critiques, however, assume a conception of utopianism that is very much at odds with the one I am seeking to write about and defend in this book, which is about utopia's role in facilitating fresh thinking about the future rather than providing detailed blueprints for change. The criticism that utopias entail a naive faith in people's capacities to effect change for the better, moreover, seems to be based on a fatalistic assumption that they are, by definition, unable to, which is absurd.

Nor, as I indicated in my earlier discussion of the role played by nostalgia in the construction of utopian visions, is it the case that utopianism is indifferent to the past. It is the nature of that past and one's attachment to it that ought to be at issue here, not utopianism's apparent disregard for it. In addition, the suggestion that utopias lack an ethical dimension is simply wrong-headed. Utopian literature is a repository of reflection on human nature – on its purposes, limitations and possibilities. You cannot get closer to moral questions than that. To argue otherwise is to betray an astonishing ignorance of the genre. Nor do utopias discourage debate. In fact, because most of them are 'open' and 'writerly' texts (Eco, 1981) that lend themselves to a multiplicity of interpretations, they tend to educate rather than delimit the experience of those who read them. Certainly, most utopias do not remotely try to command uncritical adherence. Rather, they offer their readers an invitation to reflect using a mode of 'didacticism that is at best ironic, at least self-critical' (Bartkowski, 1989, p. 12). Indeed, as we shall see in Chapter 3, it is these features of the utopian imagination, plus its paradoxical and sometimes satirical quality, that are the hallmarks of the most well known of all utopias, namely that penned by Thomas More in the sixteenth century.

'Good place' and 'no place'

The colloquial understanding of the meaning of 'utopia'is the chief problem here. This roughly defines 'utopia' as a good, but non-existent and therefore impossible, society. As most people know, this definition of the term has its origins in More's *Utopia*. The title of his book, like many of its names, is a joke – specifically, a witty conflation of two Greek words – *eutopia*, a 'good place', and *outopia*, meaning 'no place'. It thus contains deliberate ambiguity: is utopia a good place or no place – and are these necessarily the same? More's joke, as Ruth Levitas says, 'has left a lasting confusion around . . . ['utopia'], and one which constantly recurs like a familiar but nonetheless rather troublesome ghost' (1990, pp. 2–3). Undoubtedly, it spooks most contemporary dictionary definitions, all of which give both non-evaluative and evaluative meanings of the term. The adjective 'utopian', on the other hand, is usually given a derogatory interpretation: 'impracticably ideal' or 'impossible and visionary perfection'.

The elision here between perfection and impossibility is designed to help parry suggestions for change which are regarded by their critics as silly, possibly even harmful, and I have no problem with this. People of a utopian disposition sometimes need to be reminded of the danger of getting too carried away by their visions for the future. I suppose this was why the philosopher Karl Popper was so profoundly anti-utopian. He not only regarded all attempts at instituting utopia as highly danger-ous and, ultimately, leading to totalitarianism, but also saw them as being based upon a misunderstanding of the nature of scientific method and prediction. Popper's anxiety was directed, however, at a particular kind of utopianism – socialism – rather than every form of its expression. Thus, in *Conjectures and Refutations*, he acknowledges the attractions of utopianism, while drawing attention to its 'danger-ous, pernicious and self-defeating aspects' (1961, p. 358) when allied to a dialectical-materialist conception of history. For Popper, socialist utopias are always wrong-headed because it is impossible to determine social ends scientifically in the ways envisaged by those orthodox Marxists that produce them. But, then, not all applications of the utopian imagination, even some Marxist-inspired ones, for example Bloch's, start out thinking as much. In fact, the greater number of actual utopias, as I will now illustrate, neither have the same kind of content nor perform the same sort of function as utopian blueprints for the achievement of the ideal socialist society.

Categorizing and defining utopias

While More invented the specific idea of utopia, its project considerably pre-dates him. More's achievement – though of course he never intended it – was to create utopianism as a distinctive literary genre, allowing previously and subsequently published items written in the same vein to be categorized as utopian. His creative intelligence in this particular respect also encouraged others after him to exercise their own utopian imaginations in the service of political commentary and social reform.

Utopianism, as a result, constitutes a huge literary outpouring. Indeed, to quote Alain Martineau, 'so voluminous is utopian literature that a single lifetime would not suffice to read and analyze it all' (1986, p. 27). Its enormity also connects with a long history, stretching from the third century BC (Plato's *Republic* and Iambulus' *Heliopolis*), then on through the early and modern periods (Saint Benedict's *Rule*, Thomas More's *Utopia*, Francis Bacon's *New Atlantis*, Charles Fourier's *Harmony*, Karl Marx and Friedrich Engels' *Communist Manifesto*, William Morris' *News from Nowhere* and Edward Bellamy's *Looking Backward*), to work produced in the last century

(B.F. Skinner's *Walden Two*, H.G. Wells' *Men Like Gods* and Italo Calvino's *Invisible Cities*).

The diversity of utopian writing reflected in this short list of examples should be sufficient to explain why utopia eludes simple definition and easy categorization. Despite this difficulty, and at the risk of over-simplifying matters, I propose to distinguish two kinds of utopia: *spatial* utopias and *process* utopias (Harvey, 2000). Examples of what are meant by process utopias include schema for economic and welfare reform, such as twentieth-century plans for the introduction of comprehensive schooling, the development of a national health service and proposals for new forms of progressive taxation. Arguably, free-market utopianism – the attempt to increase material well-being throughout the world by means of extended capital accumulation – is the process utopia which has had the biggest impact on most people's lives during the latter half of the twentieth century. One waiting to replace it today might be George Soros' (1998) blueprint for avoiding global economic meltdown.

Spatial utopias, on the other hand, are the kinds of utopia that most people think of when they first embark on finding out more about utopianism, or when they are asked to produce a common-sense defini-tion of its character. While such utopias are not devoid of process, they place most of their emphasis upon identifying and describing a virtual or potential geographical order which is held to be perfect or much closer to perfection than any other one currently existing. Examples of this kind of utopia are Robert Owen's design for an ideal community in New Lanark, which subsequently inspired Stedman Whitewell's *New Harmony Settlement* in the USA, and the physical planning utopias of people such as Ledoux and Le Corbusier (Fishman, 1984; Hardy, 2000; Harvey, 2000).

Other spatial utopias are entirely literary in character. Reading like fictional accounts, these directly portray an admirable ideal society that indirectly criticizes an already existing one – usually the one in which the utopian author lives. This is achieved by considering the social and cultural presuppositions of this model society and the kind of life it facilitates. An example of this kind of utopia is that conceived by Charles Fourier in the nineteenth century (see Beecher and Bienvenue, 1972). This envisaged, among other things, a land of plenty in which no one went hungry – a version, in other words, of the fantas-tic *Land Of Cockaygne*, whose inhabitants want for nothing materially and where there is a super-abundance of food and drink: geese take wing ready-roasted on spits; larks fly down people's throats smothered in stew; cakes grow on trees; and wine overflows continuously.

In this case, Fourier was not envisaging concretely a society whose members would be fed magically. Rather, through the use of graphic imagery, he was seeking to mobilize among his readers a commitment to a conception of social life in which being properly fed was regarded as a basic human right. Thus, if we consider what Fourier had to say at the time about poverty and its effects as a form of allegory, the need to interpret it literally disappears. Some of his other ideas, notably about a more equal role for women within society and the nature of progressive forms of employment, admittedly were not so allegorically inscribed, and indeed turn out in parts to be prophetic. But however conceived and written up, utopias are rarely supposed to be interpreted as real places but rather, to quote Mary Midgley's sympathetic interpretation, as 'imaginative pictures of possible houses to be built' (1996, p. 24).

Practical utopian experiments in education

This is not say that efforts were not made sometimes to translate such imaginative pictures of possible houses into actual bricks and mortar, and no more so than in the education context. Indeed, where there is utopia, there are frequently to be found plans for the reinvention of education along different and progressive lines.

Thus Gerald Winstanley's mid-seventeenth-century conception of an ideal society geared to helping its citizens achieve a form of Christian redemption includes a complete education system aimed at helping people to 'discover the secrets of nature and creation within which all true knowledge is wrapped up' (Armytage, 1961, p. 25). Similarly, almost a hundred years later, the Moravian utopian experiments in community living, which at the time were chiefly dotted around various parts of Northern England, give unusually high priority to both boys' and girls' education.

Robert Owen's endeavours in New Lanark at the beginning of the eighteenth century to create a small society in which people could live without fear of crime and poverty, and with their health greatly improved, include provision for a little school house catering for all ages of children, even the very youngest, who are taught using methods that many today would recognize as 'progressive', especially the use of play in fostering learning in the early years (Clews-Harrison, 1969). Likewise, William Allen, who in 1824 forced Owen to relinquish control to him of the New Lanark schools, put up plans in the Brighton area of England designed to help its poorer citizens live more secure lives. Significantly, the first thing Allen did to implement this plan was to arrange for a school to be built. Open to pupils of any religion, his school was very innovative for the time, being equipped with a farm, printing offices and workshops – an early experiment in what today we would call 'vocational education'.

Another enthusiastic Owenite communitarian, William Maclure, operating at about the same time as Allen, established a series of schools, first in Spain, then in the USA, each of which stressed the use of Pestalozzian methods of teaching and the importance of a broad education, rather than just instruction in the 'basics', including the learning of foreign languages, mathematics and science in all its various branches. And that is not all of it, for one can go on to identify any number of nineteenth-century utopians whose practical visions for a perfected society include, centrally, improved schooling and educational opportunities – such as John Minter Morgan's (1820s) 'villages of unity and co-operation', Stedman Whitwell's (1830s) communities of 'united interests', Hugh Doherty's (1840s) 'technological utopia' and the various contributors to the early history of the English Co-operative Movement (see Armytage, 1961).

To be sure, none of these utopian experiments endured for very long, nor did they overly influence education policy and practice much beyond the localities within which they were tried out. On the other hand, they provided educators then, as now, with rich vocabularies of hope for education, indicating general directions for the improvement of schooling and adding to the range of resources available for its reform and renewal. The challenge today within education is thus not to learn to live without utopias, but rather to seek to delineate new ones which help to fuel fresh conceptions of what might contribute to the creation of schools of positive consequence for all who attend them.

Summary

This chapter has provided a working definition of utopianism – as a distinctive vocabulary of hope that helps us simultaneously critically to relativize the present and progressively to anticipate a better future. It has also argued that utopias, both in general and in the education context in particular, provide an antidote to cultural pessimism and an alternative to currently fashionable narratives of professional decline. In Chapter 3 this analysis is taken one stage further by looking in detail at one example of utopianism – Thomas More's *Utopia* – which is used to illustrate how applications of the utopian imagination can have profound consequences for the way in which we think about the practice of education and its reform.

3 Utopianism and education
The legacy of Thomas More

More's *Utopia* announced that the modern utopia would be democratic, not hierarchical. The good life would extend to everyone, in
all their pursuits – politics, work, family life, leisure and the arts.
In doing so, More democratised reason.

(Krishan Kumar)

The significance of *Utopia*

No book about utopianism can sensibly fail to discuss the significance
of Thomas More's short tract *Utopia*, arguably the most well known of
all spatial literary utopias. What is less well appreciated is the extent to
which its account is very prescient about a number of education issues
that are taken almost for granted today. For that reason I consider it
warrants in this book a whole chapter to itself. Certainly, a working
knowledge of the themes of More's utopian vision, including the
method through which he came to write it down, will enable us to
appreciate better utopia's potential to provide a distinctive vocabulary
of ultimate hope. In addition, speculation about some of the personal
factors which may have led More to write his utopia in the first place
will point up ways in which applications of the utopian imagination
can assist individuals to confront purposively and imaginatively
crises of personal and professional identity.

More's reputation

Thomas More's last recorded words – uttered shortly before his execution at Tower Hill on 6 July 1535, and spoken to his executioner – are
said to have been: 'Thou wilt give me this day a greater benefit than ever

any mortal man can be able to give me. Pluck up thy spirits, man, and be not afraid to do thine office. My neck is very short: take heed, therefore, thou strike not awry for saving of thine honesty' (Ackroyd, 1998, p. 394f.). Moments before, More is reported to have asked the few people observing his execution to 'bear witness with him that he should now there suffer death in and for the faith of the Holy Catholic Church', protesting that he died the King's 'good servant, but God's first'. Apart from a joke which More allegedly shared with one of the attending officers – it seems the steps of the scaffold were not very firm and he needed to be steadied as he climbed them, which prompted him to remark: 'When I come down again, let me shift for myself as well as I can' – he said very little else of significance (Kenny, 1983, p. 89).

The manner in which More faced the prospect of losing his life, quite apart from the factors that led him to being sentenced to death for treason – which as most people know was a consequence of his stubborn refusal to swear the Oath of Supremacy recognizing Henry VIII as head of the Church – speaks volumes about his character. For while, as particular 'revisionist' biographies of More make clear (Guy, 2000; Marius, 1984), he was not always the most 'saintly' of people, the way in which he met his death and largely lived his life was exemplary.

Being a profoundly committed Catholic and a consummate and widely respected lawyer and public servant constitute the larger part of his legacy. On the other hand, it is probably fair to say that More is most remembered for his short book *Utopia,* which he wrote many years before his rise to full public fame and eventual martyrdom. In writing this book, in which he creates a vision of an ideal society, More consolidated a specific tradition of social and political thought – one in which the dilemmas of society are considered and a prescriptive account provided of the best way to resolve them.

Since *Utopia's* publication in 1516, this tradition, which we now call utopianism, has exerted a powerful influence on the form and content of political deliberation. Its impact on education in the same period, as we learned in Chapter 2, has also been significant. Indeed, education has been a concomitant of the majority of past utopian schemes. After years of being subject to either neglect or hostile attention, there is today a renewed interest in the role of utopianism in public affairs, particularly in relation to discussions of the future of democracy and quests for an ecologically responsible society (Geus, 1999; Panitch and Leys, 2000; Wright, 1995).

Utopia and More's educational method

More's *Utopia* is a widely regarded text. Marx and Engels admired it, as did William Morris, while John Ruskin considered it to be 'the most mischievous book ever written' (Kinney, 1979). In very recent times, John Guy, the author of the latest full-length study of More, declaims it as the 'most avant-garde work of humanist moral philosophy . . . and one of the crowning achievements of the Renaissance' (2000, p. 2).

No other text within the utopian oeuvre has attracted so much scholarly attention. As the editors of a recently published *Utopian Reader* remark, 'many layers of commentary overwhelm this little book, which is almost lost under the essays and [other texts] (many longer than the original) written about it' (Claeys and Sargent, 1999, p. 77). The clamour of attention that *Utopia* has attracted over the years (Olin, 1989) is due largely both to the book's profundity and to the ambiguity surrounding More's motives in writing it, including the meaning he meant it to have. Consequently, as Anthony Kenny observes, 'one cannot imagine a medieval political treatise susceptible of such varied and contradictory interpretations' (1983, p. 102).

For those ill-acquainted with More's *Utopia*, it is important to understand at the outset that it is written in two parts, the first of which is easily passed over by those who read it today, or not known about by those who are broadly familiar with only its utopian aspects. Part 1, or Book 1, of *Utopia* takes the form of an imaginary conversation between More, a fictitious voyager called Raphael Hythlodaye (a name, jokingly, capable of being translated as 'dispenser of nonsense') and a real-life civil servant Peter Gilles, on the question of whether a philosopher should enter royal service. The conversation also provides More with a vehicle to attack specific injustices within English and European society at the time. It represents as well a backdrop to the vision of a perfect society that More goes on to outline in Book 2 of *Utopia*, a vision, we may safely assume, he wanted his readers to compare positively with the awful realities of contemporary Tudor England described in Book 1.

Book 2 of *Utopia*, the most well-known and familiar part of More's text, is a description by Hythlodaye of the distant commonwealth of Utopia or 'Nowhereland' – an island inhabited by happy, healthy, public-spirited democrats and communists where money and private property are extinct and where conventional attitudes to wealth are turned upside-down and usurped. Thus, in Utopia, gold and silver are each treated contemptuously, while all other produce on the island is collected into common storehouses, from which district officials freely draw supplies. In Utopia, doors are never locked, and anyone can enter anyone else's house at any time. Although families are permitted to eat at home if they wish, most Utopians are encouraged and prefer to have their daily meals in communal halls where food consumption is accompanied by music and educational readings. Everyone in Utopia works at a trade and takes a turn at agricultural labour. Even so, the working day is restricted to six hours in order to provide maximum opportunities for people to engage in sensible leisure pursuits, such as attending lectures, tending the garden or playing mind-expanding board games such as chess. Marital arrangements are relatively easily dissolved by divorce. Relatedly, Utopians practise complete religious toleration and have no objection to euthanasia.

Although social harmony and stability, allied to democratic practice, are the hallmarks of life on Utopia, its society is not entirely egalitarian. Intellectuals, for example, are excused from normal work regulations to help them to devote their lives to study. In addition, all higher and religious offices, including the Prince of each city in Utopia, are filled by members of the intellectual class. Other, less attractive features of life in Utopia include its travel restrictions that require people to move from place to place in groups and only with official permission. Clothing is also uniform – literally so – and made of plain undyed wool. Utopia's attitude to women is patriarchal; wives, for example, are required monthly to kneel and confess their faults to their husbands, the latter of whom are not expected to reciprocate. Children, too, are treated harshly by modern standards – close parental intimacy being discouraged, for example.

On the other hand, education is available to all in Utopia – a remarkable idea given that at the time of *Utopia's* publication the vast majority of the population in England could neither read nor write; nor were they expected to. Also extraordinary is the emphasis More places on the importance of this education being conducted in the students' 'own native language' rather than Latin, as was normally the case – possibly one of the earliest examples of an explicitly inclusive approach to curriculum development. Equally, More's concern that schooling should give as much priority to social development as to teaching the 'basics' – '[in Utopia] reading and writing are not given priority over good behaviour and morality . . . [Rather, children are inculcated] with good opinions and with attitudes that help ensure the stability of their society' (Wootton, 1999, p. 151) – anticipates, albeit very conservatively, the contemporary stress on the importance of citizenship education. Further, the emphasis More places upon encouraging educational opportunities as part of one's leisure time has the familiar ring of 'lifelong learning'. Even greater prescience is exemplified in More's hope that society would be transformed by the technology of his day – in particular, the compass, gunpowder, the printing press, movable type and paper – a sentiment that resonates with the concerns of many of today's educators to access and integrate successfully into school life the potential of the newly emerging digital modes of information storage and communication.

These few briefly described examples of the practice of education in *Utopia* represent the full extent of More's vision of the future of schooling. Well, not exactly, for what More says about education in *Utopia* needs to be viewed in the context of what he practised about it generally, and in particular in relation to the school he established in his own home for the education of his children. This context indicates clearly that More was very committed to a particular version of the educational process – namely, one that stressed the importance of education in both giving people the best possible start in life and in helping them generally to develop ways of thinking intellectually as an antidote to speaking and acting foolishly.

At the heart of More's philosophy of education was the role it should play in promoting moral probity, without which (he wrote to one of the tutors of his own children) learning brings nothing but 'notorious and noteworthy infamy'. As Guy remarks, in More's scheme of things, 'virtue and learning were . . . upheld as the way to attain piety, charity and Christian humility. Only then would a person be equipped to lead an innocent life' (2000, p. 75). More's extreme moralist stance on education led him to praise industry and condemn idleness. For More, being lazy was 'the bain of domestic, spiritual, intellectual or political life' (Murphy, 1996, p. 10). While clearly a very demanding teacher-parent, there is a wealth of evidence to suggest that More's chief means of motivating his own children to be committed to their studies was not – as one might expect – fear of his reproach (though it has to be said he was more than capable of reprimanding members of his household using very severe forms of physical punishment), but rather an interested kindliness, often leavened by a playful touch to make school work seem fun (Wegemer, 1995, pp. 81–2).

This work was delivered via a curriculum that daringly followed closely both the humanist-classical agenda and the traditions of the Catholic Church, a combination which, for others, would have seemed incompatible. Accordingly, More's children were compelled to master not only Latin and Greek literature, logic and philosophy and the works of the Church Fathers, but also mathematics and astronomy. This education experience, in contradistinction to the rest of English society at the time, was offered to both women and men. In this respect, More was an educational pioneer whose views about the importance of women's education may be regarded as 'innovative, creative and well ahead of his time' (Murphy, 1996, p. 12), though his methods need to be placed alongside an attitude of mind which led him ultimately to regard women in general as second-class citizens. It is also clear that he viewed women's education partly as one means of curbing what he saw as their innate tendency to be foolishly emotional and slothful.

In this respect, while being an imaginative educator, More was very much a product of his time, class and society. Indeed, despite More's approval of universal education in *Utopia,* his desire to promote greater equality of opportunity in practice did not embrace the likes of either his servants or their children. Further, the curriculum most admired by More was not one he negotiated, but instead was to be accepted by his children without either question or discussion. As Guy argues, 'his educational methods in his "school", notably the way the curriculum was regulated so that the texts to be studied by each member of the family were prescribed by More, suggests that there was no room for individuality or intellectual dissent' (2000, p. 212).

More's utopian 'method'

While there is no shortage of examples of the power particular utopian visions are able to exert in encouraging practical suggestions for the introduction of better systems of education, a central question still remains: namely, what is it about utopianism *as a way of thinking* about the current social order, including education, and how to change it, that gives it its dynamism and consequently continues to make it so attractive to some people?

Some answers to this question were provided in Chapter 2 which highlighted and described the most salient characteristics of the utopian mind-set, which include its relativizing of the present (Bauman); its capacity to embarrass the status quo (Eagleton); its daydreaming quality (Bloch); its effort to address positively felt absences in people's lives (Levitas); and its opening up of foreclosed desires and ways of thinking (Williams and Harvey).

More's utopian method adds to this catalogue of positive attributes. This method has two distinguishing features. First, and most important, it entails a form of literary playfulness in which readers are invited to question ideas they take for granted. It also needs to be said that, in More's case, one factor which may have influenced his choice of this way of writing about social reform was a wish on his part to distance himself from his own analysis in order to protect his emerging high public reputation, which undoubtedly would have come under close royal scrutiny if his views had been taken completely at face value. Thus More's playfulness in *Utopia* may be interpreted partly as a form of self-protection inasmuch as it 'creates a context in which [he] can say what he likes, without laying himself open to too much criticism' (Turner, 1965, p. 10).

Second, More's method appeals to a perfected, almost mythological past that connects with the hidden utopianism which, I am assuming, he thought was evident in many of his readers, in particular in the form of certain residual hopes for the future that remained unfulfilled in their lives and in society at large. To that extent, this aspect of More's method seeks to link with his readers' higher moral selves and social aspirations. But, equally, if we follow one interpretation of *Utopia* (developed in Guy, 2000, pp. 99–100), it may also be read as More's personal critique of the very humanist political programme and tradition of which he was a keen exponent and practitioner, but which he regarded as being flawed in several crucial respects. In particular, More was alarmed by, and sought to correct, its capacity to look both ways at once on the question of wealth and social privilege – on the one hand, denying 'that inherited wealth and ancient ancestry should be treated as qualifications for "true nobility"', while, on the other, defending 'the traditional link between these privileges and honour, reputation, nobility and social authority' (Guy, 2000, p. 99). More's *Utopia* thus represents a 'call to action to his fellow humanists' (Guy, 2000, pp. 101–2).

In order to make strange what is familiar, More uses a distinctive form of ironic humour-cum-satire that has the effect of leaving his readers to guess the degree to which 'the arrangements he describes are serious political proposals and how far they merely present a mocking mirror to reveal the distortions of real-life societies' (Kenny, 1983, p. 20). Either way, More's *Utopia* draws us into an imaginary perfected world, the comprehension of which helps one to think differently and critically about existing reality. Thus while some of the ideas put up by More in *Utopia* would have been recognized by many of his contemporaries as both expedient and necessary – such as the elimination of conspicuous expenditure and obstacles to distribution occasioned by stockpiling and speculating – others, for instance the abolition of private property, the toleration of religions besides Christianity, the acceptance of divorce and euthanasia and, most crucially, the equalization of labour and moves to create a more just and democratic society generally, would have knocked some of them sideways, given not only their sheer inventiveness, but the attack they implied on prevailing systems of power and privilege. As David Wootton observes, 'communism might be found in Plato, communism and labour in the New Testament, but the combination of communism and labour and egalitarianism is scarcely paralleled before *Utopia*' (1999, p. 9).

More's *Utopia*, it is suggested, was written in large part to help its readers find the necessary intellectual space to think of alternative schemas for living at a time when European society was characterized by widespread poverty, gross inequalities of income, lawlessness, and general chaos, and in desperate need of reform. More provides an indirect account of these conditions by offering a vision of an ideal society of which Europe's at the time would have appeared, by contrast, a pale reflection. The actual schema provided by More in *Utopia*, however, were not written by him in the form of a detailed blueprint for the reform of sixteenth-century Europe, but rather as an imaginative illustration – a kind of thought experiment – of what is possible if you dare to deliberate, daydream even, outside the strict confines of ways of thinking that currently have the greatest salience and influence.

Conducting thought experiments about education

While it is not my intention to commend the direct application of More's utopian method to the deliberation and construction of education policy, aspects of its approach to thinking about the future warrant serious consideration in the education context, especially if the policy issues involved connect with specific problems that have proved highly resistant to previous and current reform efforts. One aspect of More's method is particularly impressive – namely, its suggestion of a positive role for applications of the utopian imagination in enabling people to conduct thought experiments on certain negative situations that, by common consent, require urgent amelioration.

In education, one such situation relates to the current crisis affecting teacher recruitment and retention – initial teacher trainees, it appears, are proving more and more difficult to recruit to certain parts of the profession, and the morale and associated stress levels reported among its existing members are said to be very high indeed. Another relates to the poor motivation of significant proportions of under-achieving pupils in our schools, many of whom – it is estimated up to 40 per cent in some places – fail to find significance and meaning in classroom learning. Another relates to the capacity of senior school managers to construct and implement visions for their institutions that hold out the prospect of promoting increased educational opportunity and attainment for the majority rather than the few.

While aware that the very manner in which these situations are inscribed begs many questions, the central problems with which they connect are real enough, which gives rise to the question about what kind of solutions may be devised better to address them. In the UK, current favoured and fashionable solutions, as far as the teaching profession is concerned, centre on offering financial inducements to encourage graduates to enter teaching and retired teachers to return to the classroom, and the application of specific human resource management strategies – particularly those to do with performance-related pay and increased opportunities for professional and career development generally – to the circumstances of teachers in post. The levering up of pupil motivation and associated levels of attainment is being approached through a variety of initiatives which include a reinvigorated 'back to basics' curriculum, the encouragement of area-based programmes such as the Education Action Zones experiment, the establishment of specialist and 'fresh start' schools and the application of stricter regimes of school and teacher accountability via the activities of the Office for Standards in Education (Ofsted). The promotion of the capacity of senior managers to undertake their work more effectively is being addressed chiefly through new opportunities for management training such as the introduction of a specialist qualification for new and aspiring headteachers and the creation of a National College for School Leadership (NCSL).

Some of these solutions are fairly predictable, particularly those affecting teacher recruitment and management training; others, such as performance-related pay and the activities of Ofsted, while never previously tried, are controversial. Whether any of them will 'work' is too early to determine. In any event, their nature and likely success is not my concern. A different question should be asked: what other, more progressive solutions might one think of? Or, in line with the approach being commended in this chapter, if one conducted a utopian thought experiment on each of these problems, what different kinds of solutions might arise, given that utopianism is concerned both to relativize the status quo and draw out more explicitly the implications of particular respected but unfulfilled hopes and desires for education? The answer would be: many and varied.

The reason for this outcome resides in the process of conducting utopian thought experiments, which all begin with a similar question: How would social reality look if we configured it in radically different and improved terms and from a different position than is normally adopted? The form this question takes is similar to the one that the teenage Albert Einstein is said to have asked of himself as he travelled to work on the tram thinking about the nature of the relationship between time, speed and appearance: 'What would the world look like if I rode on a beam of light?' If we translate this extraordinary piece of lateral thinking into one about aspects of schooling and the problems it currently faces, questions such as the following become capable of being asked, and utopian 'answers' to them envisaged:

- What would it feel like to be educated in a school where its pupils were encouraged to play a full part in negotiating with their teachers the form, content and pace of their learning?
- What would teaching be like if learning was seen entirely from the pupils' point of view rather than largely the teacher's?
- What would teaching as a career be like if it entailed paid secondments and increased diversification of employment?
- What would education entail if it were interpreted less in terms of schooling and more in relation to the creation of lifelong opportunities for learning?
- What would schooling entail if it downgraded targets and focused almost entirely on devising and seeking ways to achieve particular *educational* aims?
- What would the school curriculum look like if its subject matter were chosen largely in terms of its contribution to helping children to live a full life rather than in relation to the short-term needs of the economy?
- What would school management entail and result in if its leaders were required continuously to legitimize their authority via negotiation with students and the teaching staff?

Each of these questions, and others like them, draw upon widely held and, in some cases, very long-standing, but often foreclosed, value positions about education – about equality of educational opportunity; about seeing its purposes in terms that are not simply utilitarian; about viewing it as a process that includes but goes beyond compulsory schooling; and about the importance of taking the learner's point of view seriously in devising and teaching programmes of study. To that extent, this particular interpretation of the utopian project serves as one means of *recovering to the forefront of teachers' and other educators' minds submerged ways of thinking both positively and prospectively about their work and about education generally.* That is to say, such questions act – as More's Utopia does for those considering the future of society – as a set of *reminders* of what the educational project is essentially about or as a collection of reflecting mirrors on the reality of current practice, exposing its limitations and contradictions.

Such reminders become very important during periods when the forces of reaction are strong and when people's capacity to innovate is seriously diminished as a result. It is not so much, as one of the critics of an earlier version of this chapter put it to me, that 'maybe the best we can hope for in the present juncture is that the utopian imagination will keep alive the memory of a lost vision, to be evoked and acted upon as and when conditions become more favourable' (Edwards, 2000), but rather that utopianism will *act in the present* to remind us of what could be achieved if we thought differently about the context of reform.

The questions listed above could just as well be the product of any progressive and socially critical educator, without that person necessarily being an educational utopian. On the other hand, such questions, if asked within a utopian frame of reference that envisions practical alternatives, may better motivate their authors to suggest ways of actually changing the world. For More did not write *Utopia* merely to stimulate the intelligence, least of all simply to amuse, but to challenge the social order of his time and to provide a fresh way of thinking about the direction of social reform. Similarly, Marx and Engels' utopian vision, *The Communist Manifesto,* is not meant to be a work of detailed political philosophy, but rather a revolutionary call to action to create a better society and in a certain image. To that extent this book is wedded to the view that utopianism in education, and elsewhere for that matter, can perform the function of being a catalyst for social change, and in ways that social criticism on its own cannot. For only when the latter is expressed in terms of concrete suggestions for improvement – which is the way of most utopias – is it capable of performing this task, (Stillman, 2001).

Utopia and crises in professional identity

There is a little more to be said about this process before ending this chapter, and it is about its implications for personal-professional development rather than societal improvement. These further reflections are prompted by certain scholarly speculations about what drove More to write *Utopia*. For sure, it is clear to most commentators that he was anxious to use this little book as a vehicle for social criticism, although a few sceptical interpretations view it as a sophisticated lampoon (Ackroyd, 1998, for example). Another suggestion is that it also served as a means for More to think through and make a decision about a professional dilemma he was confronting in his life at or near the time of the book's publication.

Anyone familiar with the life of More ought to be surprised by his apparent endorsement in *Utopia* of a set of social reforms that rub up awkwardly against how he ordinarily lived his life and the values he publicly, and no doubt privately, espoused. Anthony Kenny puts the matter very well in his observation that 'wherever we turn in *Utopia*, it seems, we find something which is contradicted in More's life' (1983, p. 98). He goes on to list some of these apparent inconsistencies in the following terms:

> Firstly, the Utopians have few laws and small regard for lawyers; More devoted most of his life to the law and became England's chief law officer. Secondly, Utopians despise precious metals . . . More, in and out of office wore a golden chain. . . . In Utopia, thirdly, it is lawful to follow . . . any religion one chooses; More prided himself on his reputation as a severe castigator of heretics. Fourthly . . . in *Utopia* divorce is permitted on comparatively easy terms; in life More went to prison rather than consent to a divorce which half the divines of Christendom thought was allowable according to Scripture and canon law. Fifthly . . . suicide in Utopia, in appropriate circumstances, is regarded as permissible and even laudable; More, however weary of life in the Tower, was scrupulously careful not to utter a word that would bring him within the death penalty and thus create a risk that he would face God before He had called him. Sixthly . . . the constitution of Utopia is radically egalitarian; More, right up to his death, behaved to the tyrant King Henry with an obsequiousness bordering on servility.

As Kenny concludes, 'it isn't difficult to prolong this list of paradoxes. How then are they to be resolved?'

One resolution (Bleich, 1984) is not to view these inconsistencies as contradictions, but instead as a set of ways invented by More to confront elliptically a crisis of personal identity brought on by a long-standing internal struggle to balance the demands placed upon him by Christian orthodoxy and the requirements of secular public life. More was torn, not just at the time of writing *Utopia*, but throughout his life, between the real-world values of his father, who encouraged him to enter the legal profession, and the values of the cloister, with its emphasis upon private learning, literature and faith. *Utopia,* on this understanding, becomes More's literary way of dealing with a terrible tension he felt in his ecclesiastical and public life – a tension intensified by the spirit of Reformation underway both in early sixteenth-century England and mainland Europe. To that extent, More's *Utopia* may constitute both a reaction on his part to the uncertain prospects of new cultural identities and a means of 'finding out what he understood about life and himself' (Fox, 1982, p. 74).

Similar uncertain prospects interpenetrate the professional lives of many teachers today as they struggle to come to terms with educational reforms that do not always articulate sensitively with their belief systems about the purposes of education and their professional role. These tensions – for example, between wanting to do the best for the children they teach in the light of the specifically *educational* aims they hold, while at the same time undertaking responsibly the new duties imposed upon them by the central state to meet pre-specified targets over which they have no control, and about which they have serious misgivings – realize crises of professional identity. These crises are often simply accommodated via the adoption of pedagogic approaches that entail a strategic mix of acquiescence and compromise (Moore *et al.*, 2002).

Occasionally, they can be recast by teachers and more fully integrated into their professional outlooks by an application of More's utopian method (see Grint, 1995, ch. 5). Specifically, teachers caught up in such crises – such as the one whose essay featured at the start of this book – might try a utopian thought experiment in which they first imagine what their perfect post and school organization might look like, which they then compare with their experience of the job in hand. Subsequently, they ask themselves if there are any gaping holes between the two that might be filled, or at least reduced by practical measures taken either by them or by other people. In this process, it is important for them not to become too hung up on the practical details of their utopia. The critical issue rather is for them to use it as a resource to clarify what is it at stake professionally in the situation that is causing anxiety because it creates a mismatch between what they would like to do and what they feel they are being compelled to do against their better judgement. This process of clarification is unlikely to provide a final solution to the dilemma it connects with, least of all throw up an immediate practical solution to it. What it may do, however, is set out clearly what is at stake, knowledge of which is a necessary condition for finding a suitable way forward.

Summary

This chapter has examined and commended the utopian method underpinning More's *Utopia*. In particular it has shown how the conducting of thought experiments about the current state and reform of education can realize imaginative solutions to some of its enduring problems, chiefly through the process of conceiving them in ways that are out of the ordinary. The chapter also pinpointed the way carrying out such experiments is able to help teachers, and public educators generally, to confront better identity dilemmas of a more directly personal-professional nature. Chapter 4 outlines a particular version of the utopian imagination – *utopian realism* – which is used a vehicle for the development of a form of Third Way politics for education.

4 Utopian realism and a Third Way for education

> The political task of social science is to . . . help define a realistic utopianism by using the knowledge of the probable to make the possible come true.
>
> (Pierre Bourdieu)

> We have to learn to discern the unrealized opportunities which lie dormant in the recesses of the present.
>
> (Andre Gorz)

Against wistful yearning

Before launching fully into this chapter, I need briefly to recall and integrate the main themes of some of the earlier ones in order to make clear the platform upon which to develop the next stage of my argument.

This book is about 'good' utopias and their application in the education context. By 'good' utopias, I mean radically progressive conceptions of the future of education that eschew mere wistful yearning ('wouldn't it be nice if') thinking in favour of positive, unusual, but ultimately practicable visions for the reform of schools and teaching and learning generally. These visions, I have argued, provide rich vocabularies of hope that help to dissolve cynical pessimism within schools by introducing a degree of optimism into public discourse about the practice and purposes of education. The sort of utopianism I am arguing for, then, is not designed to encourage deliberations about impracticable ideal states. The emphasis instead is upon identifying the forces and resources within the present social order that are capable of transforming it for the better in the future, so as to provide a significant dynamic for action in the here and now.

To repeat a previously emphasized distinction, my preferred mode of utopianism is also one that embraces a conception of hope that is 'complex' rather than 'simple', to the degree to which it is grounded in a comprehensive review of those factors which may structurally inhibit particular kinds of reform and which therefore need to be overcome if progress of a certain kind is effectively to be initiated and achieved.

This approach thus facilitates a form of 'utopian realism' in which people's 'ultimate' hopes for the future are translated into action plans that seek to push out the boundaries of what is possible on the basis of what is perceived to be realizable in the light of progressive forces already underway in contemporary society.

Real utopias

Another way of looking at all of this is to consider the state of being hopeful and the condition of being utopian as two sides of the same coin – the latter filling out and making more focused sense of the former. What I mean to suggest in particular here is that utopianism has the potential to enable the personal experience of hopefulness to be interpreted in explicitly social rather than just an individual way. I say 'explicitly' here, of course, because hope implicitly is a relational construct that assumes positive interactions of many different kinds. On the other hand, being realistically hopeful can sometimes positively refract back on being utopian by placing sensible limits on the imaginings of utopians through encouraging a form of practical rather than naive optimism. Being extravagantly utopian is mere fancifulness. For just as ought always implies can, being sensibly utopian suggests a kind of futuristic thinking that is rooted in a sensitive appreciation of the potentialities of the here and now – a form, if you like, of realized optimism or anticipatory consciousness.

These last expressions are borrowed from Bloch (1986), to whose work I made positive reference in Chapter 1. He argues, as I did then, that utopianism should be about the responsible exercise of hope in thought and action in the *present* rather than in relation to some far-off, out-of-sight realm. Indeed, Bloch is concerned to demonstrate that a better, in his case socialist, way of life is already partly manifest in the current one. Accordingly, the central political task, as he defines it, is to find practical ways of realizing this utopia in a more comprehensive and permanent form.

A similar intention informs the more recently inaugurated *Real Utopias Project*. Based at the University of Wisconsin in Madison, USA, this initiative is built around a series of workshop conferences at which between fifteen and twenty scholars discuss and respond to a provocative manuscript that 'lays out the basic outlines of a radical institutional proposal' (Wright, 1995, p. xii). At the time of writing, three such conferences have been organized dealing with reforms to the welfare state, the potential of quasi-voluntary secondary associations for the renewal of social democracy, and the viability of a form of market socialism. Others are planned on asset-based redistribution in advanced capitalism, reconstructing gender and the family, ways of making the transition to environmentally sustainable development, creating institutions for global equality, and approaches to the renewal of universalistic identities.

While the details of these existing and proposed debates are not relevant here, the point behind them is. Essentially, they are about taking seriously and deliberating the relative merits of radical alternatives to existing institutions, and about articulating this process with egalitarian values. The *Real Utopias Project*, however, is disinterested in providing detailed blueprints of such designs. Rather, what it seeks to achieve is a 'clear elaboration of the *institutional principles* that inform radical alternatives to the existing world' – an objective that 'falls between a general discussion of the moral values that motivate the enterprise and the fine-grain detail of institutional characteristics' (ibid.).

In addition, the *Real Utopias Project* is going about its work in a spirit of genuine intellectual openness which entails bringing people together from across what are often experienced as polarizing academic boundaries. Thus philosophers, political scientists, economists, educationalists and sociologists contribute to its deliberations, making it an inclusive, and-also, rather than an agonistic, either-or, initiative. Described in this way, it mimics the vision of Ludema and his colleagues who call on social scientists to move beyond their discrete critical impulses to defining simultaneously hopeful research agendas that explore the aspirations of a broad range of organizational members. They write: 'The more we enquire into and promote constructive dialogue about our ultimate concerns, the more helpful will become our theory, the more promising will become its potential for positive action, and the more we will become a source of hope to each other' (1997, p. 1045).

The Third Way Debate

Much of the agenda of the *Real Utopias Project*, and the 'and-also' manner in which it is being conducted, is discernible in the so-called 'Third Way Debate' which has been underway for the past five years in countries as diverse as Britain, Canada, the United States, Brazil, Germany, Italy and France. This debate is concerned with identifying the essential elements of a new political philosophy and economy better able than either state socialism or free-market neo-liberalism to meet successfully the massive challenges of the twenty-first century.

While the Third Way Debate in the UK has been dominated by various think tanks, notably *Demos* and *Nexus* (Halpern and Mikosz, 1998; Hargreaves and Christie, 1998), the most important individual contribution to it so far has been that made by Anthony Giddens, the sociologist and former Director of the London School of Economics. In a series of widely read and increasingly influential publications, Giddens has sought to outline the nature of a politics that goes 'beyond Left and Right' (see in particular Giddens, 1994, ch. 10, and 2001).

According to Giddens, the ideas of the free-market Right have been destructive and self-defeating. On the other hand, socialist programmes and policies in a variety of national contexts have fared no better, and are in serious disrepair. But it is not simply that these political frameworks have produced ineffectual policies. It is also the case that neither has an adequate enough understanding or diagnoses of the nature of modern society, with the result that they each start out 'on the wrong foot'. As Ulrich Beck (1997), who has strongly influenced Giddens' views, puts it: 'more and more often we find ourselves in situations which the prevailing institutions and concepts of politics can neither grasp nor adequately respond to' (p. 7). Consequently, there is a need for an alternative kind of Third Way politics that entails new thinking and innovative policies more fit for purpose than those emanating from either the traditional Left or Right, both of which are now seriously caught out of position by the changes underway in modern capitalist societies and the new challenges these pose.

Although there are some shifts of emphasis depending on national context, there is broad agreement that these challenges have arisen in relation to five fundamental transformations in modern society. The first is the growth of a globalized world economy whose activities make it increasingly difficult for governments substantially to manage national economies within their sovereign boundaries (Bauman, 1998); the second is the advance of technology and the rise of skills and information as the key drivers of employment (Castells, 1996, ch. 4), which together undermine old patterns of work and place an unprecedented premium on the need for high educational standards; the third is to do with the emergence of a new individualism in which people, in retreat from custom and tradition, are compelled more and more to constitute themselves in their own terms (Beck, 1992, ch. 5); the fourth is the breakdown of the old structures of the life cycle on which much of this century's welfare and education are founded (Giddens, 1994, ch. 7); while the fifth is the rise of ecological politics and the growing demand that environmental problems should be better integrated into social democratic deliberation (Beck, 1998, ch. 12).

Responding to these changes, however, does not entail the abandonment of values ordinarily associated with the political Left. On the contrary, Giddens is concerned to articulate his political Third Way with a set of common foundational values which most socialists would readily acknowledge as central to their own political outlook. These include freedom, equality, emancipation and co-operation. The difference is that Giddens translates these values within a social democratic rather than a democratic socialist political framework.

But more than that, and significant given the focus of this book, Giddens inscribes his political vision in terms that are recognizably utopian. Specifically, and in a way that resembles the objectives of the *Real Utopias Project*, Giddens refers to his approach to developing a Third Way in politics as an example of 'utopian realism'. By 'utopian', Giddens means to draw attention to the fact that his vision is out of the ordinary; by 'realistic', he means to stress that his ideas are rooted in actually existing social processes, notably the rise of new individualism, and related to common foundational values.

To that extent, Giddens' utopia is neither a fine-grained portrayal of an ideal society nor a detailed blueprint to realize one. On the other hand, it does invite consideration of the need for and content of a new form of social democracy, thus satisfying the visionary qualities ordinarily associated with applications of the utopian imagination. Anthony Barnett (1997) puts this point slightly differently: 'Giddens' utopian realism seeks to handle change by working backwards from the goal. The goal is a disclosure of hopes and objectives, not a blueprint, a plan, a god or a final solution' (p. 271).

Like Barnett, Giddens is anxious to avoid the charge that what he is proposing is realizable by definition. Instead, what he offers is 'a critical theory [of society] without guarantees' (1994, p. 249) – that is to say, a radical thesis about the nature and future of political economy which is critically insightful, but without entailing historical inevitability. Thus, in contrast to classical Marxist utopianism, Giddens' less deterministic conception of the future eschews intrinsic solutions. Nor does it propose any social force, least of all the organized working class, as the inherent bearer of a better society. On the contrary, in the latter connection, Giddens cautions us from thinking that any group today 'has a monopoly over radical thought or action in a post-traditional social universe' (1994, p. 250) where life for the majority is no longer constructed against the backdrop of a single grand narrative, but rather invented as a means to its own ends.

This process, as Beck (1992) stresses, removes society's members from 'historically prescribed social norms and commitments', while simultaneously re-embedding them into a 'a new type of social commitment' (pp. 127–8) in which they are required to 'produce, stage and cobble together' their own biographies (Beck, 1998, p. 33). Indeed, with ever-decreasing direct lines to what kind of life is most worth living (what Bauman, 1992, p. xxv) intriguingly calls 'collective utopias'), everyone now is required to contemplate and decide between a 'plurality of scenarios' (Giddens, 1998a, p. 28), entailing a mode of 'generative politics' (Giddens, 1994, p. 15; 1996, p. 232) that 'breaks open and erupts *beyond* the formal responsibilities and hierarchies' (Beck, 1997, p. 99) and which 'seeks to allow individuals and groups to *make things happen*, rather than have things happen to them, in the context of overall social concerns and goals' (Giddens, 1994, p. 15).

'Making things happen' in this way requires the state to take on new roles. In particular, it must underplay its function as monopolistic provider of welfare services and strengthen its capacity to create the necessary regulatory frameworks within which public, private and voluntary sectors co-operate. This entails providing the necessary infrastructures to ensure that socially excluded groups can act as full citizens and thus take greater control over the nature and direction of their own lives.

Giddens associates this form of political behaviour with a series of specific policy innovations which include reducing the power of the executive in British politics and strengthening its accountability; promoting experiments in direct democracy and community-based approaches to crime prevention; encouraging co-parenting and mutual rights and responsibilities; replacing traditional poverty programmes with community-focused, participatory initiatives; and creating new forms of positive welfare that invest in the prevention of failure rather than in its amelioration.

Objections to the Third Way

Not surprisingly, the space carved out by Giddens here has not gone unchallenged. Chantal Mouffe (1998), Decca Aitkenhead (1998), Perry Anderson (1994) and Stuart Hall (1998), for example, all insist on the continuing necessity to configure political activism around the traditional antagonisms of Left–Right. Hall, in particular, is hostile to the implication in the Third Way that radical politics can proceed in the absence of conflicting interests: 'a project to transform and modernise society in a radical direction which does not disturb any existing interests and has no enemies is not a serious political enterprise' (1998, p. 10). Eric Hobsbawm (1998), Martin Jacques (1998) and Will Hutton (1998), on the other hand, argue that Giddens' Third Way lacks a sufficiently robust political economy because it accepts capitalism largely as it is and assumes as a consequence that growing inequality can only be, at best, mollified. While Ted Benton (1999) attacks the very foundations of Giddens' analysis, claiming that he has misunderstood the nature of globalization, argued against a caricature of the socialist project and failed to take seriously into account the on-going importance of class as a significant source of social identity.

But these dismissals of Giddens' attempt to plot a Third Way are not altogether fair. In actual fact, Giddens nowhere denies the continuing salience of the Left–Right distinction in terms of its capacity to elevate successfully issues of equality and emancipation. What he does insist is that it 'hasn't now got the purchase it used to have' (1998, p. 41), and that the 'equation between being on the Left and being radical no longer stands up' (ibid., p. 46). It is not fair either to suggest that Giddens considers there to be no longer any conflicting interests. One has only to read his account of the challenges faced by ecological politics to see that this is not true. What Giddens does deny is that there are hosts of conflicting interests that, by definition, cannot be reconciled. His view is that most can be, even though the outcome (as, say, in the North of Ireland) may not amount to a *final* resolution. The point too is that in a world of greater interdependency, certain interests may find it actually expedient to seek *rapprochement* with historic enemies. Nor is Giddens complacent about the importance of reforming capitalism so that the needs of the less well off can be more effectively attended to. Again, in actual fact, he suggests a number of practical ways in which the global economic order could be made better and more humanely regulated, including the establishment of an Economic Security Council within the United Nations.

Benton's seemingly more devastating critique also falls away on close inspection. Besides being based upon a radical distortion of Giddens' actual position on globalization, it embraces a highly contestable assessment of both the reality and potentiality of class politics. Where it seems strongest is in its objection to Giddens' refutation of socialist politics which, admittedly, is narrowly focused on its failure to manage effectively national economies. However, while Benton is right to point up the significance of variants of socialism other than the revolutionary kind, he fails to explain how any of these might in practice address adequately the major social transformations of our time. Associationist socialism is undoubtedly attractive as a mode of social living, but it is hardly a satisfactory means for running a modern society as a whole.

But this is to stray from the main point which, is not to defend the detail of Giddens' conception of the Third Way, but rather to point up its potential for encouraging critical reflection on the limitations of the here and now and on ways to improve the situation. As such, it offers a model exercise in both asking and prompting the asking of questions. Nowhere does it pretend to be putting all the right questions, least of all every question that has been asked about the future of social democracy. Accordingly, there is a sense in which some of Giddens' critics may have misunderstood his project, which is not to provide a new totalizing analysis, but to offer a heuristic framework within which alternatives can be generated and their relative merits deliberated. To that extent, Giddens' promulgation of the Third Way represents not only an illustration of the kind of thought experiments we encountered in Chapter 3, but also a particular diagnosis designed to help reconstitute the social world and assist in the reconfiguration and resolution of its problems.

The Third Way and Labour's education policy

While there is more than a family resemblance between the ideas of the Third Way and the *tenor* of the British Labour Party's recent project to modernize itself, close inspection of what Labour has actually sought to achieve since becoming the government of the UK in 1997 suggests that its politics in power are not easily recognizable as beyond Left and Right.

Certainly, in education, what seems to have happened is the generation of a curious, even incoherent, 'pick and mix' of policies that possess both Old Left and New Right characteristics. For example, Labour has retained much of the previous Conservative emphasis on the education marketplace, including increasing the number of specialist schools and encouraging the growth of more faith-based ones. On the other hand, educational it has sought ways better to redistribute resources in order, in its terms, 'to benefit the many not the few'. Looked at as a whole, though, it is difficult to discern in Labour's programme for school reform much, if anything, that is distinctively or significantly 'beyond' what has been tried before. As Power and Whitty remark, 'New Labour's education programme generally follows the path of the New Right' (1999, p. 543). But worse, they conclude, its 're-labelling the process of marketization and privatization under the new more fashionable discourses of mutuality and partnership does little to address the very real concerns about access to and adequacy of provision that emerged during the [previous] Conservative years' (ibid., p. 545).

The exception may be Labour's Education Action Zones (EAZ) policy, which it specifically links with the politics of the Third Way (Hodge, 1998). The context for this initiative is Labour's national strategy for tackling the combination of local needs and priorities associated with poverty and deprivation. A key aspect of this strategy has been to make available additional resources to parts of Britain where these problems cluster through the setting up of so-called local 'action zones' – for employment (which seek to provide new forms of training to help the long-term jobless move into either self-employment or neighbourhood regeneration work); for health (which aim to foster health promotion initiatives in areas of cumulative disadvantage); and for education (which are designed to combat low levels of school achievement and social exclusion in localities where both feature strongly).

EAZs, however, are conceived in particular as 'the standard bearers in a new crusade uniting business, schools, local education authorities and parents to modernise and improve education in areas of social deprivation' (DfEE, 1998). As such, they are regarded by the Labour Government as a significant blueprint for 'the future delivery of [all] . . . public services in the next century' (Rafferty, 1998).

At the time of writing there are seventy-three EAZs operating in England, implicating about 10 per cent of the nation's schools. Based in areas of relative deprivation, both urban and rural, they typically cover between fifteen and twenty-five institutions, usually made up of two or three secondary schools and their 'feeder' primary and special schools. Each EAZ runs for an initial period of three years, with the possibility of an extension to five years if satisfactory progress is made. The overall strategy for each zone is set by an Education

Action Forum (EAF), a managing body made up of the main partners which more often than not include a local education authority, the schools themselves, a business interest and parental and other community representation. The EAF draws up an 'action plan', the key planning document for the zone, which includes targets for each school taking part, and for the EAZ as a whole. Strategic direction, as well as day-to-day management and financial responsibility, fall to the zone's project director. Each zone receives between £500,000 and £750,000 funding each year from the government. In return they are expected to draw in up to £250,000 from private sector partners.

While some of the EAZ policy's features resemble closely earlier UK experiments in addressing persistent low educational achievement, notably the Educational Priority Areas (EPAs) policy of the 1960s and 1970s which allowed local authorities to discriminate positively in favour of schools operating in poor areas, there is much that is novel and arguably Third Way about what it is seeking to achieve. Its effort to promote a variety of partnership arrangements to encourage new forms of educational provision certainly breaks the previous monopolistic control of school provision previously enjoyed by local education authorities. The policy's commitment to across-the-board experimentation in curriculum provision, which entails zone schools being allowed to opt out of teaching the government's normally prescribed National Curriculum and its innovative approach to educational self-governance are also noteworthy. Indeed, in the latter case, if they fulfilled their potential, EAFs could provide a significant site of generative politics within which individuals and groups, representing a wide variety of interests, deliberate and decide upon local education policy and provision. On this understanding, Labour's EAZ policy appears to be both utopian and realistic – 'utopian' insofar as it represents a significant break with the past; 'realistic' to the extent that this break is sensitively connected with an appreciation of what can actually be achieved in the present.

But what is the policy like in practice, beginning with its impact on educational outcomes? There are undoubtedly indications that schools in EAZs are starting to see improvements in some of their results. Eight EAZ schools were recently awarded the Ofsted 'Gold Star' for outstanding performance in challenging circumstances, for example; and eighteen of the hundred 'most improved' primary schools between 1997 and 2000 are also in EAZs; and in two zones there are reported signs of a reduction in poor attendance and truancy since the policy was introduced (DfES, 2001a). These data are encouraging.

But, equally, other early evidence, some of it emanating from the government's own school inspection teams (DfES, 2001b), also suggests that not all the schools in particular zones experience the benefits of zone status. Thus, while primary schools operating within EAZs often show increased levels of academic productivity, secondaries fare less well on similar measures. More worrying are data that suggest EAZ schools – whether primary or secondary – do not out-perform academically similarly deprived schools not covered by an action zone (Manseu, 2002). The chief problem here it seems is the failure of successful zone schools to disseminate satisfactorily to their neighbours the policies and practices which helped them to lever up their standards. Moreover, further data (which I helped to collect as part of a team of researchers conducting a national evaluation of the policy) indicate that the majority of early EAZ curriculum innovations, while new to the zones concerned, are not new to the school sector as a whole. Indeed, our research has found many instances of EAZ funding being used to prop up and extend pre-existing initiatives, few of which could be regarded as radical departures from currently available curriculum provision and delivery as anticipated by the policy's advocates.

A form then of First Way conservativism rather than Third Way innovatedness seems to have taken hold in many places, an outcome not altogether surprising given the nature of the action plans drawn up by many of the original successful applications for zone status. A review of the content of the first twenty-five of these by Riley *et al.*, for example, draws attention to the extent to which only a small minority of them seek to break with convention: 'there are few radical proposals to make major changes to the national curriculum' (1998, p. 7). Relatedly, while many of the initiatives proposed have the potential to raise standards, the actual 'targets for improvement (literacy, numeracy, attendance, parental involvement and expectation, etc.) are conventional ambitions in local education authorities and schools across the country' (ibid., p. 11). To that extent there is, the reviewers conclude, little that is new or ground-breaking here. There is also the worry that, whatever happens, the scale of resources dedicated to the initiative is proportionately far too small (Plewis, 1998) and the fear that, without a strategy for generalizing good practice, it will be difficult for it to have any more than immediately local benefits. Even locally, as Power and Whitty observe, 'it is hard to see how any gains can be sustained once the funding stops' (1999, p. 10).

In some cases, even where business involvement is taken into account, the anticipated funding from that source has not been substantial. Certainly some of the zone directors we interviewed expressed

disappointment and even frustration at the low involvement and investment of the private sector in their particular zones, many businesses
appearing reluctant to donate or invest significant amounts of cash.

To a large extent, the degree of business involvement, of course,
is dependent on factors outside the control of any given EAZ. By
definition, EAZs are situated within economically depressed areas
and, in many cases, are thus hampered in their fund-raising efforts by
the dearth of large local employers. However, we found that the presence of large national or multinational partners within an EAZ is no
guarantee either that their contribution will be equally significant.
The result is that there is a huge disparity in the amounts of funding
raised by individual zones from local businesses. Hallgarten and
Watling's (2001) review of the audited accounts for fifteen zones in
their first year, for example, points out that, while one EAZ successfully
raised £400,000 from business in six months, the other fourteen
brought in only £550,000 in total from the same source. More recently,
Mansell (2001) found that only twelve zones out of the seventy-three
presently operating have secured the expected £250,000 per year
from the private sector, with most sponsorship taking the form instead
of contributions 'in kind' rather than cash.

Beyond Education Action Zones

EAZ policy thus has some way to go to warrant the reputation of
being *quintessentially* a utopian and Third Way educational reform.
In theory, as already suggested, it does have some Third Way characteristics and utopian pretensions – it is community-based and focused; it
seeks to promote experiments in devolved forms of educational governance; it embodies a new approach to providing education; and it
stresses inclusivity.

What is particularly lacking, however, is any sense that the policy as
conceived connects systematically with any of the fundamental changes
underway in contemporary society which were outlined above. Put
another way, it is not entirely clear what the policy's concrete proposals
are designed to achieve other than to lever up some rather commonplace education standards. This is a worthy objective – no doubt
about that – but what is it *for*? In other words, with what view of
the overall purposes of education does it articulate? We are not told,
except that there is a strong implication that raising standards in this
way will in some way contribute to increasing pupils' employability
and consequently impact positively on economic growth. But these
connections are neither necessary nor arguably likely. To that extent,

EAZs seem to be a policy that largely takes for granted what it should be either spelling out or subjecting to critique.

This raises the question about whether there are any other, possibly better, ways of translating the promise of Giddens' utopian realism into practical policy for education. Tom Bentley's (1998) much heralded educational utopia as outlined in his book *Learning Beyond the Classroom* may be nearer the mark, particularly as its starting point is a recognition of the long-term impact of the so-called 'information age' on work, employment and education.

Here, in ways reminiscent of the *Real Utopias Project*, is an attempt to work out some policy initiatives having first identified certain basic first principles. In Bentley's case, this entails initially thinking more about the ends of education rather than its means. Specifically, he argues that education should strive, not so much for equality of educational opportunity as for the provision of opportunities for learning that foster autonomy, responsibility and creativity. In the course of arguing in this way, Bentley introduces a heresy: that good teachers and excellent schools cannot help more than a minority of deprived children to escape their background. This 'romantic image' of teachers and schools transforming pupils' lives, he says, is largely illusory: 'It relies on the myth that individuals can buck the system and transform their destiny, but ignores the fact that these individuals are the exception. They leave many others, with similar potential for achievement, behind.' Thus what is required is much less emphasis on conventional schooling and an increased stress on enabling people to access a variety of opportunities to learn.

Bentley's vision is much better grounded in the actual order of things than is the EAZ policy. For example, unlike the latter, he acknowledges at the outset that the global economy is now characterized by the almost instantaneous flow and exchange of information, which suggests the need for new modes of access to learning and new forms of knowledge creation. There is not a hint of such an analysis in the EAZ initiative where the stress is much more on structures and teacher and school improvement. These new modes of access, Bentley says, must be 'demand-led and individualised, employing information and communications technologies, weak control structures and network forms of organisation'.

On this reading of his book, Bentley is an unashamed modern de-schooler – someone who envisages a future learning society in which people learn in a variety of ways and places and at different times, but not necessarily in school. Indeed, more and more learning, he says, will have to take place in the contexts where knowledge is actually used and valued, rather than, as is largely the case now, in recognizable sites of instruction. What is required, he concludes, is a new 'public knowledge infrastructure', accessible not only through schools, but via homes, libraries, firms, universities, community centres and voluntary organizations.

Within such an infrastructure, curriculum delivery would have to be 'individualised, emphasising less of the standardised consistency of institutions and examination boards, and more the rigorous coherence of disciplined individual learning'. Bentley's specific proposals include: the right of parents to claim back the cost of a child's education to create their own school; the option for pupils to engage in community- rather than school-based learning at age 14; assessment of educational performance by a greater range of external bodies than at present; and the use of existing school buildings for a wide range of community purposes.

This is a strikingly utopian vision for the future of education. It also embodies many more Third Way features than Labour's EAZ policy. In particular, it takes very much on board the idea that people should be helped to construct their own learning choices rather than have them provided on a plate. But is it realistic? As a blueprint for reform, it probably isn't. But that is not its purpose. Similar again to the *Real Utopias Project*, it elaborates institutional *principles* rather than a grand design. And, like Giddens' utopianism, it prompts one to ask new questions, in this case about existing and future structures of educational provision, and about the purpose and nature of teaching and learning in a network age. And, like Giddens' approach, it is a vision grounded partly in already existing practice, such as the new infrastructure of lifelong learning that is slowly taking shape in this country through such measures as the National Grid for Learning and the Individual Learning Accounts initiative. Of course, these are neither well-developed experiments nor ones to which the UK Labour government has as yet linked much public money, and they are largely targeted at those who have left behind the compulsory phases of education. However, having said that, they provide a hint of what might be possible elsewhere, and on a much bigger and grander scale, and thus fuel public optimism about the possibilities for educational reform.

As I have argued from the outset, optimism of the will in this con- text is no bad thing. Indeed, in much the same way that students work better with teachers who have high expectations of their poten- tial, so societies with a strong, positive sense of the future bring out the best in people. Of course, it may all still turn out badly, but that is what it is like to live in an uncertain world where history offers no guarantees and where we are compelled to work with what there is.

Summary

This chapter has outlined and commended a particular version of the utopian imagination – utopian realism – which entails envisaging possible futures in terms of detectable trends in actual social development. It has also assessed the merits for education policy of a recent attempt to translate this kind of utopianism into a mode of practical politics known as the Third Way. The three chapters that follow will examine how the perspective of utopian realism can be usefully applied to three areas of education policy and practice, beginning in Chapter 5 with its implications for leadership and management in schools.

5 Utopian educational management and leadership

Hope is catalyzed and sustained when people come together in mutual relationship to inquire into their highest ideals and to construct a collectively desired future.

(James Ludema)

Managing staff in schools

While the words of the pessimistic teacher whose essay began Chapter 1 echo throughout this book, they resonate more so at this point in my argument than probably at any other. The essay ends, it will be recalled, with its author offering up a challenge to those senior staff in his school who presently manage his work to give him the support he needs in order to help restore the 'loyalty and sense of vocation' he once had.

While the essayist does not say what kind of support he specifically needs to rehabilitate his commitment to the job in hand, we can make a number of intelligent guesses about what it might include. Campbell and Neill (1994), for instance, consider that heads and other managers in schools need to identify and protect better their staffs from those work demands that are not central to the task of promoting student learning. As they state: 'A major function for [them] . . . is to find ways to limit teacher workloads by identifying priorities for their schools, and filtering out demands which make the most conscientious teachers' workloads unreasonable' (p. 177). Clearly, there is a lot more to be done than this, and much of it is to do with finding ways to re-motivate those teachers who feel both disillusioned by the work they are expected to do and put off by the school-specific contexts in which they are required to undertake it.

Fortunately, the extensive literature on how best to manage staff in schools is littered with helpful practical suggestions about this, ranging from proposals that senior managers should pay proper attention to the overall work environment, to advising them to recognize and reduce role conflict and ambiguity. Much of this literature also stresses the way in which managers should set challenging tasks for their staff, but not ones that threaten their competence to undertake them. Equally, considerable store is laid on the value of collegial models of school decision-making in increasing motivational levels (Furukawa, 1989; Riches, 1997).

Linda Evans' empirical study of what actually motivates teachers and helps to increase their job satisfaction also provides a number of useful guides for school managers. In particular, she stresses the importance of 'motivational school leadership', entailing headteachers acknowledging explicitly the efforts and talents of colleagues in the form of positive feedback (1998, pp. 45, 136). She also draws attention to the fact that, when schools and their teachers share broadly the same philosophies of education and professional values, staff morale is higher than in situations where the opposite is the case.

In addition to developing their human resource management strategies in the light of these suggestions, senior school managers may need to reflect on what is currently known about some of the working practices of those commercial managers who take seriously the need to create occupational cultures that are worker-friendly and which encourage high levels of innovation.

The starting point in all of this is a truism: that happy employees are better workers than miserable ones. Research undertaken by Dominic Swords (1999) of the Henley Management College puts this more directly: 'there appears to be a positive correlation between an atmosphere of human playfulness in the workplace and the improvement of innovative activity and creativity.' Conversely, creativity is unlikely to thrive in organizations with a blame culture or in ones dogged by territorial rights. Other research, this time based on an eight-year-long study of a hundred companies, fills this out further. It concludes that 'an employee's satisfaction with their work and a positive view of the organization, combined with relatively extensive and sophisticated people-management practices, are the most important predictors of the future productivity of companies' (West and Patterson, 1999, p. 22). The people-management practices referred to here include those that concentrate on enabling staff to enjoy their work rather than feel oppressed by it; that encourage questioning and thinking; and that develop co-operation through investing in social capital and mutual trust within the organization.

This list is particularly relevant to school management philosophy as currently practiced which many teachers consider lays far too much

vision as a utopia — "agreed among staff as a whole" —
x without structural democ !

76   *Hope and Education*

stress on performativity linked to the achievement of prescribed performance indicators – often expressed as 'targets' – that are used to 'measure' individual productivity. While such measurements have a place in schools, their utilization is likely to realize positive outcomes only if those to whom they are applied feel confident that the results will be used to help them to improve, rather than as a means to draw attention to their weaknesses.

Vision-building

One way of building within schools this sort of trust, and, at the same time, enhancing the morale, motivation and hopefulness of teachers is through the process that has become known in the education management literature as 'developing a shared vision'. The specific literature on this topic is huge, and no attempt is made here even to summarize it, other than to point up some themes that connect with the arguments of this book.

The 'vision' of a school is an expression of its central values, beliefs and aims which provides a 'mental picture of [its] preferred future' (Caldwell and Spinks, 1992, p. 37) – a kind of utopia, in other words. Where it has been agreed among staff as a whole, rather than imposed on them from above, a school's utopian vision for itself has the potential to provide all concerned with a spur to positive action. In ideal circumstances, it can thus motivate staff to make changes in line with a common ideal for the evolution of the school. Crucial in this process is the progressive nature of the vision that needs to be at least one step ahead of reality for continuous improvement to result. This gap between 'reality as it is' and 'reality as one would like it' (in Bloch's terms, the 'yet-not conscious'), it seems, provides the necessary creative tension that is both a source of institutional hopefulness and a means to transform the present. To have this effect, such visions, like utopias, have to be bold, optimistic and ambitious. They must also anticipate a way forward as well as prefigure the future in reasonably concrete – utopian realistic – terms.

The sources of visions of this kind are many and varied. Nanus (1992) helpfully identifies four basic elements from which they can grow. First, he argues, visions require 'information' to answer the questions that arise as their constituent parts are deliberated and forged; second, they need 'values' to guide the selection of what is considered to be most worthwhile; third, they must have a 'framework' of ideas about how the internal environment of the hoped-for school and the world outside will finally link up with each other; and, finally, they require 'insight', by which Nanus means the imagination of those involved to develop new patterns of relationships among old elements.

Thinking experimentally about school leadership

It is about the last of these elements that I want now to encourage reflection. Specifically, I want to ask and answer two related questions: What sorts of relationship within schools are more likely to bring the hope back into teachers' practice when it is lacking, and how can senior school leaders and managers contribute to creating them?

To answer these questions, I propose to undertake a utopian thought experiment about school leadership which starts out from a different set of premises from those frequently found in the management practices of today's schools. In this experiment, you will be asked to envisage a school where its leaders 'invite' staff to undertake specific duties, rather than instruct them to; where staff are not so much 'held to account' for their work as 'trusted' to undertake it; and where staff are supported professionally as individuals, rather than treated as a homogeneous group with common uniform needs.

The thought experiment takes the form of an empirical case study of the leadership capability, style and practice of Maire Symons, the head-teacher of a Catholic secondary school located in the West Midlands region of England. The case study, which I contributed as part of a wider investigation of the current state of leadership capability in English Schools (Earley *et al.*, 2002), offers an *operational image* of how this particular head successfully exercises her leadership responsibilities in her school, which is articulated with a particular conception of what makes her approach to school leadership such an effective one and, ultimately, utopian in its scope and consequences.

That conception is derived from some of the academic literature on school leadership – notably those sources (e.g. Purkey and Novak, 1990; Stoll and Fink, 1996) that stress the important *psychological* function that *communicating positive invitational messages* has for enabling individuals and groups to build and act on a shared vision of enhanced learning experiences for pupils. It is also informed by the suggestion (made by Gronn, 1999) that leadership status in schools cannot be assumed, but rather is more often *conferred by followers* when they perceive their values being fulfilled in the outlooks and actions of those occupying positions of seniority. But, before elaborating all of this, I need to outline the school context within which Maire Symons exercises her leadership responsibilities.

The school context

Bishop Challoner School, which is situated in a densely populated and socially and economically deprived suburb of Birmingham, is a fifty-year-old voluntary-aided comprehensive school and specialist sports college providing education for just over a thousand boys and girls aged 11 to 18 and employment for over seventy teaching and support staff. Nearly one-third of its pupils come from ethnic minority backgrounds. More than the national average number of its total intake is entitled to free school meals; the same is true of those identified as having special educational needs. Although the school recruits from the full ability range at age 11, the proportion of higher attaining pupils it admits is relatively small, a consequence partly of the market competition from a local selective grammar school which successfully 'creams off' the more able.

While plans are well in train to improve the school's accommodation, including providing a new sixth-form block and accompanying teaching rooms, staff and pupils do not presently enjoy the opportunity to teach and learn in purpose-built, state-of the-art premises. On the contrary, some teaching spaces are cramped, while others are housed in uninviting temporary buildings. Even the school's sports facilities, which partly service its sports college status, are limited.

Limitations in its intake and accommodation, however, do not constrain Bishop Challoner's capacity to provide a quality education. On the contrary, where these factors might in other contexts be used to excuse a lack of success, they seem to act as a spur to the staff to seek improvement remorselessly, as evidenced by the fact that pupils make very good progress from entry to the school in Year 7 to the end of Year 9. Indeed, during the past five years, the upward trend in standards attained in national tests by its pupils has risen incrementally more sharply than that achieved nationally. The result is that the school has grown in popularity, with year cohorts expanding by fifty pupils on average since 1991. Little wonder, then, that a recently published Ofsted inspection report on the school felt able to conclude that it was 'providing excellent value for money' and 'achieving very well', with 'good capacity to improve even further'.

While the school's 'capacity to improve' cannot be accounted for by exclusive reference to the efforts of its headteacher, Maire Symons' leadership capability and invitational style have a good deal to do with it. Certainly, all with whom I came into contact during the course of conducting my case study spoke well of the manner in which she was able simultaneously to lead from the front *and* foster a climate in which staff felt confident to suggest new ideas and take initiatives to see them though, and without constant reference back. This central aspect of Maire Symons' leadership capability resonates with the idea mentioned above that leadership status in schools is sometimes less to do with delegating responsibility and much more about encouraging 'followership'.

Leadership philosophy

For Maire Symons, the meaning of school leadership is best summed up in her detestation of unnecessary bureaucracy, which is reflected in a wish to discourage meetings in her school that serve only to communicate information rather than make decisions; and in her desire to flatten hierarchies, which is embodied in her efforts to build leadership capacity throughout the organization via an affirming invitation to everyone at all levels to work hard and take responsibility for their actions.

Leavening this process is Maire Symons' *generous energetic expectation,* in the course of which she inspires all with whom she makes contact – teaching and support staff, pupils, parents, governors, visitors (including myself) – by the way she enthusiastically 'walks and talks the job'. This entails, as she puts it, providing 'clear direction for the work of the school'; 'encouraging an effective learning environment and good relationships throughout'; and fostering 'a consultative style of management' and associated 'clear lines of communication and effective team membership'.

This interpretation of Maire Symons' leadership role is one equally and easily recognized by colleagues and pupils who, without too much prompting, freely comment positively on her 'heart-and-soul' and 'hands-on' attitude to headship; on her 'dedication and commitment'; and on her 'supportive' approach generally. This high estimation of her leadership capability and practice is endorsed by Ofsted, which describes them as 'excellent, enthusiastic and vibrant'. How all of this is routinized and practised is the concern of the rest of this chapter. But, first, some further theory.

Cultural aspects of organizational change

While getting things in good order is probably a necessary condition for achieving organizational change, it is never sufficient. For radical organizational change within schools – configured as a utopia – is as much about the way managers and the managed think and work together as

about the way the organization officially operates and is formally struc-
tured. Indeed, the methods by which radical change might be achieved
organizationally have to be as firmly rooted in a cultural re-evaluation
of the shared assumptions and beliefs which help to reproduce what
goes on in a school, as in rethinking and reforming the explicit mechanisms which help to make things happen within it. By this I mean that
the interplay between the concepts and belief systems with which the
staff of a school think and the social relations to which these give rise
structure their perceptions of what is practicable and appropriate. To
that extent, the culture of a school sets the stage on which continuous
valuations of what is possible are made.

As Stoll and Fink (1996) point out, these evaluations are in significant part based upon how staff conceive of themselves professionally
and the ways in which managers reinforce and challenge the perceptions they have of what they can and cannot do. Central to this process
is the exercise of choice; that is to say, staff make choices about the
ways they make sense of their experience and, crucially, the sense
they make of themselves. This choice is constrained by the nature of
their experience of work. If this entails a considerable amount of negative interactions with people and things, then the chances will be that an
individual's concept of self will be a diminished one; equally, if that
person's interactions with the world are mostly positive, then this is
likely to result in an enlarged vision of what is possible.

The implications of this for the management of organizational
change in schools are clear enough. Changing schools – improving
schools – cannot only be about making changes to their structures,
though that is likely to be part of it. It is also about *changing the
people* who work in them – specifically teachers' values and outlooks
that, together, help to constitute their current sense of themselves *as
teachers* and what they are capable of achieving. This suggests that,
in orchestrating school improvement, considerable attention needs to
be focused on finding ways of helping all concerned to celebrate,
evaluate and, where necessary, revise the basic ideas they think and
act with. It suggests too that, in building teachers' self-confidence to
attend critically to their perceptions of themselves and of school reality,
attention also simultaneously needs to be given to the *manner* in which
this process is initiated and undertaken.

Invitational leadership

This is where the theory of 'invitational leadership' (Stoll and Fink,
1996) comes into play. For it reminds us that people are more likely

to feel able and willing to embrace change if the way in which they are requested to do so by their managers is interpreted by them as welcoming and affirming. Such positive invitations tell them that they are able, responsible and worthwhile. Disinvitations, on the other hand, are experienced by those who receive them as 'uncaring, demeaning, devaluing, intolerant or discriminatory' (p. 109).

According to Stoll and Fink, invitational leadership has four characteristics – it is *optimistic*; it is *respectful*; it is *trusting*; and it is *supportive*. To appreciate better how each of these can be translated into practice, I want to look closely now at the way in which Maire Symons exercises her leadership capability, beginning with her sense of optimism.

Optimism

Anyone who has been a member of a sports team will recall with enthusiasm the role good captains play in enabling inspirational performance. There is insufficient space here to comment on what this entails, least of all to provide examples, other than to remark that good captains are frequently those who are able to lift the spirits of their teams on specific occasions through the exercise and sharing of optimism, even when this may be unwarranted. Certainly, good captains are not those who admit defeat in advance of competition. True, they may think privately that the odds are stacked against victory, but they act publicly in front of the rest of the team as if this is still a possibility. Similarly, even when defeat is staring the team in the face, and even when the final result goes badly against it, the good captain seeks to maintain morale and encourage the idea of 'living to fight another day'. Such captaincy is thus utopian.

Invitational leadership is premised upon utopian optimism of this kind. Optimism takes a variety of guises in Maire Symons' case, however. First, she is infectiously enthusiastic about her role and the work of her school. Consequently, she is publicly never downbeat or defeatist. She has what is often described as a 'can-do' approach to headship, which is exemplified both in what she says and does. It is also evident in her body language. She speaks quickly, urgently sometimes, and readily makes eye-contact. She listens to what people say, often refracting back to them her own version of what they are talking about.

Second, Maire Symons is a solution-driven manager rather than a problem-preoccupied one, and consequently has high professional expectations of herself, which she translates into a positive view of the potential and capability of all those with whom she works. Indeed, she holds very high expectations *of others*, and consciously seeks out ways of reinforcing what they can do rather than drawing unnecessary attention to their shortcomings. She is an optimist of the will, continuously drawing attention to and acknowledging publicly the achievements of her staff, while seeking out ways to tap better into their potential for growth and development. Maire Symons thus speaks *with* staff, not *about* them, affirming their worth and encouraging their efforts. She uses the 'we' much more than the 'I'.

The result is that staff at all levels enjoy their work and have a strong sense of purpose about it and professional efficacy generally. They feel invited to perform at their best, as significantly do the pupils with whom I came into contact, many of whom commented positively on the 'aim-high' culture of the school, which they applauded and sought to internalize in their working patterns. Of course, Maire Symons is not entirely responsible for all of this; the staff are responsible for it as well. In fact, she successfully feeds on and into a professional climate that pre-dates her appointment at Bishop Challoner. Her achievement has been to consolidate and extend this positive attitude and foster a more inclusive leadership style than the one prevailing before her arrival. The starting point for this is a shared system of values. Maire Symons' professional values – which are to do with doing one's best for *all* children irrespective of their backgrounds and measured abilities – are her colleagues' values as well, all of which makes it easier for them to give full assent to her leadership. Indeed, their followership, and the achieved leadership status that Maire Symons enjoys as a result, derives centrally from her ability to inspire *collective* confidence in the validity of a vision which she and the staff hold in common. It also derives from the sense staff have of her honesty, competence, perspicacity and far-sightedness. In other words, she models in her conduct about the school the very values to which the rest of the staff adhere and that they expect her role to embody.

Far-sightedness, of course, is an aspect of optimism. School leaders who possess it keep asking 'Why not?' and 'What next?' Maire Symons is one such leader. Rather than collude with the idea that what is currently needed in schools is a period of stability, she subscribes to the notion that change is an inevitable feature of the educational world that has to be anticipated and managed. She also encourages risk-taking among staff, being receptive to staff experimentation, while keeping a watchful eye out for any unintentional negative consequences of their enthusiasms. Relatedly, Maire Symons recognizes that she must sometimes protect her staff from the worst effects of reforms generated from without, or at least hover above the crises they sometimes create, in order, on their behalf, to see things in the round and in a broader perspective and act accordingly. Consequently, she is not afraid to be decisive when others may be unsure of how best to proceed, which of course is a further quality that one associates with an optimistic disposition. So is humour, and much of this is in evidence in the routine face-to-face encounters Maire Symons has with colleagues, which are always friendly and frequently upbeat, and sometimes jokey. Certainly she smiles a lot and avoids looking downcast in public, even when she may be feeling quite the opposite.

Respect

The invitation Maire Symons offers her staff is not only an optimistic one; it is also respectful. This respect is manifest in her general civility, politeness and courtesy. It is also reflected in her invitation to discuss issues, even to the point of encouraging dissent about them.

It is noticeable how often she takes time out to say 'thank you' to colleagues for the work they are doing, and they appreciate it. During staff briefings she rarely fails to find an opportunity to draw attention to and offer thanks for the efforts of an individual member of staff or a group. This is not contrived; nor is it over-planned, to the extent that it appears based largely on memory rather than prepared script. In this connection, it is impressive how much information Maire Symons holds in her head about what staff are doing on behalf of the school. To that extent, she appears to be in tune with what is going on around her, and only infrequently does she need to be briefed about what her colleagues have been up to.

Maire Symons' respect for her colleagues is particularly noticeable in the way in which she conducts meetings, where colleagues are continuously invited to contribute their views ('What do you think we should do?'; 'Do you think that is a valid point?'; 'Is there anything we have left out?'). She never calls for a vote, preferring to take soundings from around the room and then offer a view about the best course of action if one has not already been suggested. She builds consensus through discussion, and sometimes argument, particularly when the issue at hand is contentious. Her leadership on such occasions is profoundly democratic, however. For sure, she often knows where she wants to go, but she forges agreement beforehand about what needs to be done through participation. Moreover, meetings chaired by Maire Symons minimize the transactional and maximize the transformational

– that is, they invite participants to engage in problem-solving rather than in the passive receipt of information – and she builds leadership capacity by acknowledging the expertise of others to whom she routinely hands over control of the meeting. She trusts them, in other words.

Trust

Trust is a necessary condition for bringing about change in any organization. Certainly its absence fosters states of mind antithetical to taking risks and thinking and acting differently, in particular, cynicism and suspiciousness. Little surprise then that trust is one of the premises of invitational leadership. For invitational leaders not only act with integrity, they also trust others to behave in concert with the organization's mission. The result is a willingness on the part of such leaders to divest themselves of their own power and to allow that of subordinates to grow.

In Maire Symons' case this is achieved by being receptive to the suggestions of others and sharing her leadership with them. This is particularly evident in leadership team meetings where individual members of staff are caused to exercise full responsibility for specific areas of school policy – for the curriculum; for financial management; for performance management; and for school improvement. This entails taking decisions; collecting data; developing schema; and acting as advocate. Maire Symons does not simply defer to each of these people's greater expertise during leadership team meetings; she reinforces and reintegrates what they offer. In particular, she strategically invites everyone to pool knowledge for the benefit of the meeting and the school as a whole. The result is that there is an absence of empire-building and a great emphasis on a form of mutual appreciation that is manifest in the careful, courteous way in which individual reports are listened to and discussed. Such encounters lack rancour and exude goodwill. Consequently, they invite all those present to participate fully, thus adding to the school's stock of social capital.

Support

Social capital, which is the crucible of trust, refers to the ability of people to work together for common purposes. Invitational leadership contributes to its growth by the way in which it cares for and supports the efforts of others. At Bishop Challoner this project takes a variety of forms. One entails linking closely the school's professional development plan with its overall strategy for institutional improvement. Accordingly, professional development monies at Bishop Challoner are used chiefly to build up the capacity needed to move the school forward on its medium and long-term aims. Another is to make the effort to better identify and strengthen staff weaknesses and limitations, which includes making more of particular relevant expertise when this is either being obscured or allowed to falter.

This last effort is one that Maire Symons is fond of making, to the degree that she has a reputation for knowing about the skills of individual members of staff which currently do not feature in their work role, but which if drawn into the equation would enhance the individual's job satisfaction and performance as well as contribute positively to the life of the school. She is, in other words, good at profiling the strengths of the people with whom she works, especially the members of the leadership team. As an invitational leader, Maire Symons is thus continually on the look-out for ways of better deploying her staff and pushing them on to success. Young teachers beginning their career at Bishop Challoner particularly comment enthusiastically about this aspect of her leadership capability, which they see as promoting their interests in the wider cause of advancing the school's.

The shift from control to efficacy

Invitational leadership entails a shift away from a leadership paradigm based on power and control to one based on the encouragement of greater overall professional efficacy. To exercise invitational leadership successfully requires headteachers to possess the disposition and desire to invite others to take responsibility for their own actions. The effect is to divest the authority conventionally inscribed in the head's role. Indeed, there is a sense in which the more teachers accept this invitation, the less there is a need for headteacher leadership. Followership rather than leadership, becomes more the norm. Accordingly, invitational leadership, of the kind practised by Maire Symons, is profoundly *educational and democratic*. Arguably, it also helps its practitioners to move beyond the merely managerial and procedural, including the constraints and expectations of the education marketplace, towards a style of leadership that is person-centred and learning-focused.

But can it be nurtured and developed among aspiring and existing school leaders? Are not the qualities upon which it is based ones that are caught rather than taught? Are not such leaders born rather than made? How can optimism, a central feature of invitational leadership, for example, be nurtured? The strict answer of course is 'not easily'; but that does not mean it cannot be learned. For, while undoubtedly some people are more prone 'to look on the bright side' than others, optimism is not an innate disposition. Indeed, some of the most optimistic of people are depressives who have learned through therapy various repertoires to counter their pessimistic constructions of themselves and their circumstances. Similarly, health workers, who successfully care for the very sick, have learned through training to be positive and encouraging. What this suggests is that optimistic school leadership could be nurtured too, along with the capability better to respect, trust and support other people.

Summary

This chapter has documented and recommended a particular conception of school management, at the centre of which is a utopian vision about the possibility of effecting major organizational reform within schools through the exercise of an 'invitational' mode of school leadership. The justification for this leadership style has been made through an exemplary case study of the working practices of an English headteacher who motivates and mobilizes staff commitment to change by being optimistic, respectful, trusting and supportive. The case study also points towards the possibility that such leadership capability may contribute to the increased democratization of schooling, a topic which will be addressed more comprehensively in Chapter 6.

6 Deliberative democracy and utopian school governance

> Democracy is not so much about where the political is located, but how it is experienced.
>
> (S. Wolin)

Democracy in *Utopia*: participation and deliberation

Although the eradication of private property is the single most important aspect of Thomas More's Utopia, the emphasis he places on democratic governance is also noteworthy, if somewhat less radically rendered. Typically, More's *Utopia* embraces contradictory stances about how Utopia should be governed: at one turn, it commends a form of authoritarianism in the way it sets out the need to impose specific limitations on people's freedom of movement; at another, it advocates the establishment of a variety of elective local assemblies which nominate individuals to serve as senators on a council of the whole island headed by a chief executive.

These contrasting ideas do not prevent More from proposing the use of secret electoral ballots to secure his ideal republic, a voting procedure that would have struck many of his sixteenth-century readers as very unusual indeed. Equally striking are the range of measures he recommends about the proper conduct of political decision-making, which include the suggestion that discussion of resolutions by the senators should never be undertaken by them on the same day they are first presented (in order to give them adequate thinking time before making their arguments), and the proposal that they should normally arise out of debate conducted initially at the very local level.

While More's utopian vision takes democratic state-craft very seriously, other utopians have gone down quite different routes in how they conceptualize the good governance of their ideal worlds. The utopian visions of some anarchist theorists, for example, eschew the proceduralist and statist approach commended by More. Thus the nineteenth-century Russian political philosopher Peter Kropotkin conceives of a society without government as we know it, arguing that its members' conduct should be regulated, 'not by laws, nor by authorities, whether self-imposed or elected, but by mutual agreements . . . and by the sum of social customs and habits' (quoted in Geus, 1999, pp. 96–7). Similarly, the twentieth-century American anarchist Murray Bookchin describes a utopian society in which 'face-to-face' communication and citizenship, enacted within very small-scale cities, is the preferred ideal.

Although, unlike More, these anarchists do not prescribe in advance the sort of institutions needed better to govern society – indeed they deny the need for them – they share with him a commitment to the linked ideas of participatory and deliberative democracy. By 'participatory democracy', I mean to refer to a process of political activism that includes but moves beyond its 'representational' counterpart. While the latter points up the important role to be played by elected assemblies, councils and parliaments in running the affairs of society, the former directs attention to the sorts of contexts in which political deliberation, including voting, takes place, and who takes part and in what ways. By 'deliberative democracy', I mean a way of operating politically in which matters of policy difference are resolved wherever possible by discussion, and which proceeds from and is constituted by particular values which, crucially, include a commitment to telling the truth and a respect for other people and their views.

In the context of this book, the idea of participatory democracy presses home the need to reflect on how best to foster better collective decision-making about education – locally, regionally and nationally – to ensure that the services which schools provide comprehensively meet the needs of pupils, their families and their teachers. Indeed, what will be argued for in this chapter is the need to extend a form of participatory and deliberative democracy to more and more people in the education context, an idea inspired partly by Norberto Bobbio's injunction that 'the criterion for judging the state of democratization achieved . . . should no longer [just] be to establish who votes, but where they can vote and how' (1987, p. 56).

Accordingly, while I am aware that political deliberation – the business of hammering out and amassing the evidence in relation to social means and ends – does not always require particular democratic *structures* – for 'there is both totalitarian democracy and political democracy' (Crick, 1964, p. 64) – certain kinds of democratic *processes*, it seems to me, are crucial to determining fairly who gets what, when and how. Thus defined, democracy and distributive justice are inseparable in my scheme of things.

This leads me to ask if you know or can guess the identity of the author of the following words:

> A democracy is more than a form of government; it is primarily a mode of associated living, of conjoint communicated experience. The extension in space of the number of the individuals who participate in an interest so that each has to refer his own action to that of others, and to consider the action of others to give point and direction to his own, is equivalent to the breaking down of those barriers of class, race and national territory which kept men from perceiving the full import of their activity.

They are John Dewey's, of course, derived from his classic treatise *Democracy and Education* (1963, p. 87). The fact that they were first published nearly ninety years ago helps to explain their jarring sexism today. However, if we ignore Dewey's gender blindness and concentrate instead on the essence of what he is saying about the nature of democracy *as process* you will appreciate better, as well as anticipate fully, what I want to write about the politics of education in this chapter.

Essentially, I will argue that the good governance of education requires us to rethink radically how it is presently engaged with democratically. This entails, after Dewey, extending to ever-increasing numbers of people opportunities to deliberate the ends of education and the means of providing for them. To that extent, I shall be arguing for a form of educational politics that reasserts the importance of collective responsibility over and against the atomized decision-making favoured by advocates of the education marketplace. On this understanding, developing greater equality of educational opportunity requires the creation of better ways for people generally 'to express local [educational] needs and share in the decision-making about provision to meet them' (Ranson, 1994, p. 129). Mine, then, is a utopian vision in which is expressed a desire – a hope, if you like – for a different, better, democratic way of being generally, and a way of doing things more democratically within education in particular.

Trust, social capital and the politics of education

Involving people in this way however is not only a necessary condition for the development of greater equality of educational opportunity. It is also a crucial element in the process of reconstituting and revitalizing civil society as a whole in order both to countermand the excessive powers of the interventionist central state and to foster people's confidence in their ability to direct their own lives (Keane, 1988). Robert Reich, previously Secretary of Labour in the first Clinton Administration (and now Professor of Social and Economic Policy at Brandeis University), puts this far better than I do:

> The real job of re-knitting the social fabric has to begin where the threads start. That means getting more people involved in politics at the local level. There are too many people in positions of authority who are not leading, and too many at the grass roots resigned to the way things are.
>
> (Reich, 1998)

Of course, all of this is easier written down than done. On the other hand, as I will indicate below, there are certain other features of contemporary society that provide the basis for building up the very kind of reinvigorated democratic involvement being suggested here. These, however, cannot be taken advantage of fully without creating new institutions of democratic practice that entail a significant degree of experimentation in democratic involvement.

In the education context, it will require the introduction of modes of school governance that are genuinely inclusive in the sense that they encourage and enable previously silent and sometimes silenced minorities to 'have their say' and exert influence. It will also require a greater emphasis to be placed on the local 'government' of education at the expense of the local 'management' of individual schools. As I see it, the latter is essentially about the practical implementation of policy; the former about deliberating policy priorities and evaluating their consequences. Arguably, the Local Management of Schools (LMS), as currently configured and practised in schools in England and Wales, is over-preoccupied with management and insufficiently absorbed in government – or what I prefer to call the politics of education.

The starting point for the argument of this chapter, then, is that this trend needs to be reversed – specifically, that schools aspiring to greater inclusivity need to be governed seriously and not just managed effectively. Indeed, management without government is simply

Trust & social capital

managerialism, which is an insufficient basis upon which to build genuinely inclusive schools. Rather, the development of inclusive schooling goes hand-in-hand with a politics of education that is genuinely participative. Indeed, the politics of education, as I will seek to define them in this chapter, are as much about the constitution of new educational communities as about what takes place within them.

While my starting point is clearly a highly partisan one, it is underpinned by an influential trend in contemporary social theory as well as people's ordinary and intergenerational experience. The theory is about the building of trust through investing in social capital; the experience is about the benefits of getting on better with one another: 'Trust is the expectation that arises within a community of regular, honest and co-operative behaviour, based on commonly shared norms, on the part of other members of that community' (Fukuyama, 1995, p. 24). Relatedly, social capital points up the ability people have to work together for common purposes in groups and organizations (Coleman, 1988; Putman *et al.*, 1993).

The social capital perspective, which is based on a diverse body of empirical evidence, emphasizes the extent to which companies, towns, industrial regions and even national economies can all function more efficiently and fairly when there is a rich endowment of mutually respectful, trusting relationships prevailing between people. There is evidence too that an increase in trust and social capital impacts positively on people's health and the social environment generally, including rates of crime and violence (Wilkinson, 1996).

All of this follows because an increase in trust and social capital facilitates active dialogue, optimal sharing of relevant information and the maximum of willing participation (Ranson and Stewart, 1998). In short, social capital, articulating with trust, is the essential ingredient that promotes high levels of confidence and goodwill – two easily recognized precepts of the education project. In addition, because both 'involve the certainty that relationships and the expectations they involve will continue to exist' (Hirst, 1997, p. 79), trust and social capital facilitate change. Where neither exists, or each exists only superficially, as we learned in Chapter 5, people tend to become suspicious and cynical – states of mind antithetical to taking risks and thinking and acting progressively.

Trust and social capital then are very significant political phenomena with powerful social virtues. They concern the way in which citizens behave and interact with each other. A necessary condition within society for increasing trust and social capital must be opportunities for its citizens to participate with each other in respectful dialogue to achieve shared goals. The greater the variety of citizens who can so participate, the greater will be society's stock of working social capital. This latter point means that equality of communicative status has to be extended to the greatest variety of participants in order to maximize the virtue and gains from social capital. This requires genuine tolerance among individuals and an absence of social exclusionist institutions.

Thus stated, this is so obvious that one wonders why it needs to be written down. Common-sense experience tells us that 'government and co-operation are in all things the laws of life' (Ruskin, 1898, p. 102); and that competition, by definition, must pervert the pursuit of common ends. One measure of the incredible ideological impact then that marketized versions of schooling have had on the public consciousness is the degree to which they have come to seem the norm rather than an aberration. No small wonder therefore that social scientists working on education topics are sometimes accused of telling us what we do not wish to hear, but which we know to be the case. Perhaps what is really happening on such occasions is that an old, very submerged memory trace is being reactivated.

Take, for example, the work of Furstenberg and Hughes (1995) that highlights the way in which accumulations of social capital influence for the better school staying-on rates among African-American young people. Or consider Fuchs and Reklis' (1997) research which concludes that the strength of parental relationships and the influence of other social networks contribute positively to children's 'readiness to learn'. Nothing unfamiliar here, I wager. And, closer to home for British readers, ponder Willms' (1997) research in Scottish Catholic schools which suggests that the success these institutions enjoy may be in part dependent upon strong levels of social capital within the communities they serve. This finding, and all the others, connects very well with much of what emanates from the school improvement movement. It also illuminates the significance of research that works from the other direction, such as Martin and her colleagues' (1996) investigation of the impact of new forms of education management which pinpoints the degree to which isolation from networks of local support can prejudice seriously the efforts of schools in contexts of disadvantage to improve.

Countervailing forces and the challenge of social reflexivity

The relationship between increasing educational opportunity and access and the rebuilding of trust and social capital is then a synergetic one: each not only needs the other to exist, but their actual interaction realises an enhanced effect – a revitalization of part of civil society through greater democratic involvement.

I suspect though that this sort of play on words will not make much impact on those persons who think that, however cleverly democracy in the educational context is reinvented, it will remain a minority pursuit of the relatively well educated and prosperous who will do their usual best to advance their own interests at the expense of the majority. Indeed, my views at this point have been especially subject to this kind of criticism from some of my colleagues who work in the field of the sociology of education. They argue that certain structural features of society, in particular the way in which power is unevenly distributed in favour of the already privileged and well-off, make it highly unlikely that democracy can be reinvented along the lines I propose.

My reply to this sort of objection takes the form, first, of an acknowledgement that there are, of course, many grounds for being justifiably pessimistic about the possibilities for radical social and educational reform. The history of education is littered with many progressive measures that simply failed to live up to their advocates' ambitions. And current circumstances, notably growing disenchantment among some young people about the value of education altogether, make it difficult sometimes to be other than despondent about the future of mass schooling.

But this admission is quickly followed, second, by an insistence that there are none the less reasons to remain optimistic. One of these derives from the obvious enough idea that, if human beings could have invented the habits of thought and power that structure the present unequal educational order, they can be imaginative enough to undo and change them. Another is the fact that certain features of contemporary society make this more likely now than at any other period. The features I have in mind here are the expansion of 'social reflexivity' and the process of 'detraditionalization', terms that feature strongly in the work of Giddens, to which earlier reference was made in Chapter 4.

Both terms are chiefly elaborated in Giddens' book *Beyond Left and Right*, where he writes of 'the emergence of a post-traditional social order' in which 'traditions have to explain themselves, to become open to interrogation or discourse' (1994, p. 5), rather than just taken for granted. This process is one aspect of the most basic change affecting contemporary societies – 'the expansion of social reflexivity', by which Giddens means the manner in which, today, individuals routinely draw on and filter all sorts of information in the course of constructing and living their lives.

No longer hidebound by tradition, people now actively shape their own lives, which are experienced 'experimentally', and in ways hitherto inconceivable: 'tradition more and more must be contemplated, defended, sifted through, in relation to the awareness that there exists a variety of other ways of doing things . . . Everyday experiments become an intrinsic part of our daily activities, in contexts in which information coming from a diversity of sources . . . must in some way be made sense of and utilised' (Giddens, 1994, p. 83). These processes contribute to the growing confidence of citizens to challenge authority, particularly that vested in political and state institutions. They also provide the necessary conditions for encouraging increased levels of participation in the political sphere.

Central to Giddens' position at this point is his notion of 'dialogic democracy'. Dialogic democratization, Giddens is quick to emphasize, is not an adjunct to liberal democracy. Rather, 'it creates forms of social interchange which can contribute substantially, perhaps even decisively, to the reconstructing of social solidarity'; nor is it a process centred on the state, but 'refracts back on it' by encouraging debate within the sphere of the liberal democratic polity about political means and ends. This deliberative ideal, as Ranson reminds us, starts from the premise that 'in society we are confronted by different perspectives, alternative life-styles and views of the world' (1994, p. 110) and that the primary function of democratic institutions is to help people resolve the conflicts to which these differences give rise. Resolution conflict of this sort requires, says Ranson, a 'fusion of horizons', an outcome which is possible only in 'ideal speech contexts' in which the 'participants feel able to speak freely, truly, sincerely'.

However, Giddens does not see dialogic democracy as being the same thing as an ideal speech situation: 'I don't presume . . . that such democratization is somehow implied by the very act of speech or dialogue. The potential for dialogic democracy is instead carried in the spread of social reflexivity' (1994, p. 115). In addition, because dialogic democracy presumes that dialogue provides 'a means of living along with the other in a relation of mutual tolerance' (ibid.), it carries with it the possibility of building new communities of common interest:

> The advance of social reflexivity means that individuals have no choice but to make choices; and these choices define who we are. People have to 'construct their own biographies' in order to sustain

a coherent sense of self-identity; yet they cannot do so without interacting with others, and this very fact creates new solidarities.

(Giddens. 1994, p. 126)

A politics of presence and recognition

But the fostering of dialogic democracy requires more than a clarion call, however sophisticated its mode of expression. It needs further theorization, and appropriate opportunities for it to flourish. Here, again, I am indebted to the insights of Ranson and his colleagues (Nixon *et al.*, 1996, 1997a).

In considering the contexts and aspirations of a revitalized democracy, they draw on the work of the feminist political scientist Anne Phillips – in particular her argument in favour of a 'politics of presence' (Phillips, 1993, 1995). Her analysis, and their use of it, reminds us of one line of important meaning surrounding terms such as 'representative' and 'representation', both of which are commonly linked to the democratic process – the idea that democracy aims to 'make present'. In this connection, Phillips presses upon us the need to encourage modes of deliberative democracy that respond positively to 'calls for equal representation of women with men; demands for a more even-handed balance between the different ethnic groups that make up . . . society; demands for the political inclusion of groups that have come to see themselves as marginalised or silenced or excluded' (1995, p. 5).

According to Phillips, the major challenge facing those concerned to democratize democracy is therefore 'to generate that more comprehensive understanding that validates the worth of each group' which entails, in turn, an approach based on the assumption that 'difference must be recognised and equality guaranteed' (Phillips, 1993, p. 160). The 'politics of presence' requires, then, a 'politics of recognition' (Taylor, 1994) – that is to say, a politics which both recognizes the equal value of different groups within society and acknowledges their worth, or what Giddens has termed a 'positive appreciation of difference' (1994, p. 130).

On this understanding, becoming implicated in the process of deliberative democracy is not only a matter of being 'made present', but having that presence recognized as both different and equal. As Nixon *et al.* conclude, 'such a citizen is to be distinguished from those who, although recognised as equal and different, have no "presence"; for example, members of a group that, although valued and celebrated, have no representation in the main forums of the polity' (1997b, p. 21). Recognition of this kind requires an act of will of the kind that entails a willingness, in this context, 'to stay on the lookout for marginalised people – people whom we instinctively think of as "they" rather than "us"; people with whom we should try to notice our similarities' (based on Rorty, 1989, p. 196).

Enhancing deliberative democracy   *– little politics*
+ associationalism

Theory is one thing; establishing and strengthening the spaces in which deliberative democracy may be practised is something else altogether. What is needed therefore at this point are some embodiments of how the form of active citizenship I am arguing for can be worked out on the ground, and then some discussion of their applicability to the educational context. My argument, however, still needs to be buttressed by a little more theory, this time theory about the kinds of mechanisms needed to support a more participatory approach to decision-making.

Two sources guide my thinking at this point: Anna Yeatman's (1994) discussion of 'little polities' and Paul Hirst's (1993, 1994) analysis of 'associationalism'. In similar vein to Phillips and Taylor, Yeatman argues in favour of a conception of citizenship that 'works with and accepts difference' (1994, p. 86), recognizes the contested nature of public purposes and enables different voices to 'make present' their cultural identities and material class interests. In practical terms, this entails the creation of 'little polities' or dialogic spaces for negotiation between service delivers and users that offer opportunities for citizen participation and deliberative action with regard to public institutions.

Hirst's theorems complement Yeatman's. These seek to show how to democratize and empower civil society further through the principles of 'associative democracy'. Opposed to both state collectivism and pure free-market individualism, associationalism claims that liberty and human welfare are best served when as many of the activities of society as possible are organized by voluntary and democratically run 'associations'. Hirst argues that associationalist relationships can be built by citizens' initiatives freely formed by committed individuals. I would argue that they can also be helped along by the central state. Either way, the associationalist principle is best thought of as a 'supplement to and a healthy competitor for the dominant forms of social organisation', in particular representative democratic institutions such as local authorities. To that extent, it does not prefigure a future society as such, but serves rather as 'an axial principle of social organisation; that is, a pattern of organising social relations that can be generalised across sectors and domains of social activity' (Hirst, 1993, pp. 131–2).

In reality, as Whitty (1997) observes, such associations are likely to take various forms, with some being created by the state, while others develop out of local initiatives. On the other hand, the huge growth and proliferation of self-help groups in recent years is testimony enough to the suggestion that they will spring up despite assistance from the centre or other official sources (see Giddens, 1994, p. 120f.). Even so, and mindful of Yeatman's strictures about the need to work with and accept difference, it is important to recognize and overcome some of the exclusionary implications of Giddens' deliberative model.

Iris Young has drawn attention to some of these. In particular, she focuses on the ways in which power itself can enter into the very form of communication entailed in deliberation. I hinted at this earlier on, only to skate over its significance because of my faith in the reality and potential of social reflexivity. But this was a serious sleight of hand – for there is a real difficulty here. As Young puts it: 'The deliberative ideal tends to assume that when we eliminate the influence of economic and political power, people's ways of speaking and understanding will be the same; but this will be true only if we also eliminate their cultural differences and different social positions' (1996, p. 122f.).

Deliberation is neither neutral nor universal. On the contrary, 'the deliberative model of communication derives from specific institutional contexts of the modern West – scientific debate, modern parliaments and courts' (ibid.), all of which privilege an agonistic style of speaking and 'expert' users of it. Speech that is assertive and confrontational is here more valued than speech that is tentative, exploratory or conciliatory, which must favour male speaking styles over female ones. Indeed, there is a growing literature that confirms this empirically (see e.g. Mansbridge's (1991) study of state legislators in the USA and Deem *et al.*'s (1995) investigation of the working patterns of school governing bodies in the UK, each of which illustrates the degree to which, in formal settings, men talk considerably more than women and take on leadership roles more often).

The norms of deliberation also privilege speech that is formal and general – that proceeds from premise to conclusion in an orderly fashion. This form of articulateness has to be learned and is culturally specific. Relatedly, deliberation favours dispassionate and disembodied forms of discourse, identifying (falsely) objectivity with the absence or near absence of emotional expression. These different modes of speech, Young argues, 'correlate with other differences of social privilege. The speech culture of white middle-class men tends to be more controlled, without significant gesture and expression of emotion. By contrast, the speech culture of women and racial minorities tends to be more excited and embodied, more valuing the expression of emotion, the use of figurative language, modulation in tone and voice, and wide gesture' (1996, p. 124; see also Henry, 1990, who discusses the role played by anger and emotion in African-American styles of public debate, and Tannen's, 1992, study of the contrasting ways in which women and men talk and their different uses of conversation).

Young concludes from these considerations that, for it to succeed, deliberative democracy requires a broader, more explicit theory of communicative competence than is often assumed by its advocates – one which appreciates that a mannered mode of speaking is not the only, or sometimes even the best way of arguing things through to a political decision. This leads her to recommend the adoption of modes of communicative interaction that facilitate trust and 'lubricate on-going discussion', in particular what she refers to as *Greetings* which are conciliatory and caring. Young also commends *rhetoric* (that which 'announces the situatedness of communication') and *storytelling* (the sharing of narratives that 'exhibit subjective experience to other subjects' and reveal 'sources of values, culture and meaning') as other important adjuncts to conventional modes of speaking politically which, when used in imaginative combination, can strengthen the discursive inclusivity of political deliberation and thus the ability of people better to solve collective problems. Similarly, Gambetta (1998) develops a strong case for not excluding the passions in deliberative democracy. People who are too cool, analytical and impartial, he argues, may generate distrust or simply fail to rally people around issues. On the other hand, as Johnson (1998) illustrates, if discussion involves parties who seek to challenge one another at a fundamental level, it may lead to an 'intellectual war' in which they tear each other apart.

While the brevity of my review of these arguments causes serious damage to their actual subtlety, I hope I have written enough about them to illustrate their importance in the process of thinking about how best to improve the actual dynamics of democratic involvement. I am none the less conscious that Iris Young's analysis is stronger on the nature of an expanded notion of communicative competence than on suggesting new contexts and conditions for its implementation.

As for the latter, consideration needs to be given to schemes for equalizing the resources available to different associations. At its most basic, resource-poor citizens' associations will need to be capacitated so that they can compete effectively with resource-rich special interests (see Cohen and Rogers, 1995, and Schmitter, 1995, for some specific and detailed suggestions on this). As for the former, it is important to note that the exclusionary implications of 'scientific' debate, as identified by Young, are reproduced in actual *places* – assembly halls, courtrooms, council chambers and the rest – and at strategic *moments*. Arguably, such settings and times, and not just the deliberative practices with which they are associated, are not always conducive to conflict resolution, the sharing of information or the eliciting of people's opinions.

Consider for a moment the conduct of a typical annual meeting of parents that all school governing bodies in England and Wales are required to convene and you will appreciate what I mean. These occasions (as reported by Deem *et al.*, 1995) are often stultifyingly boring, poorly attended and inhibiting of discussion. What ought to be an opportunity for a healthy exchange of views about the school's work and its plans for the future is, in effect, an institutionalized monologue in which the Chair of Governors and other officials do most of the talking and the parents, for whom the meeting has been called, do all of the listening.

But such passive involvement is not particular to the annual meeting of parents – it is an immediately recognizable feature of many official public gatherings. All the more reason, therefore, to reflect on the implications of ideas currently being developed within local government to increase people's level of involvement in, and thus the quality of, democratic practice. These include experimenting with approaches to the conduct of public meetings that get away from the conventional division between 'platform' and 'audience', the use of local referenda, deliberative opinion polls, citizen monitors, mediation groups, citizen's juries, standing citizens' panels, consensus conferencing and other modes of 'direct democracy' such as electronic debate (Budge, 1996; Stewart, 1996a, 1996b for details).

Of course, as I have already stressed, in developing the sorts of intermediate bodies listed here we clearly need to give careful consideration to their composition, nature and powers. Certainly they will need to respond to critiques of the gender and ethnic bias of conventional forms of political association, and develop for this purpose a serious politics of both presence and recognition. They will also need to foster more inclusive modes of political deliberation of the kind envisaged by Iris Young and others, bearing in mind that some of the procedures I have identified above, notably mediation groups and consensus conferencing, assume them already.

Education Action Zones and democratic participation

But how does this kind of abstract theorizing connect with current education policy and practice in the UK? Well, in some ways very badly, as my story about the annual meeting of parents has indicated. On the other hand, there are new developments in the governance of schools which may suggest that a corner can be turned in the process of making them both more inclusive and better governed. I am thinking in particular here, as in Chapter 4, of the UK Labour government's Education Action Zones (EAZs) experiment.

The context for this experiment, as I have explained, is the government's national strategy for neighbourhood renewal that aims 'to deliver policies that actually work for areas of acute deprivation' (Blair, 1998) – policies affecting decaying housing, vandalized public spaces, high rates of youth unemployment, substandard schools and unhealthy lifestyles.

Central to the working out of this particular experiment on the ground are the activities of local Education Action Forums (EAFs), which are required to steer strategically the work of each zone and provide a democratic context for discussions and decision-making about what should be given priority by its participating schools. To ensure appropriate representation, EAFs are urged to include in their membership parents, teachers and representatives of the governing bodies of participating schools, and figure-heads drawn from the local business and social community.

Our research on EAZs, which has enabled us to observe two EAFs at close quarters over an extended period, suggests not only that the decision-making processes of zones are too often opaque, but also that they lack a significant dialogic, and ultimately democratic, dynamic. EAFs, remember, are the arenas in which zone strategies and resource allocations are supposed to be agreed among the various stakeholders. However, the reality of forum meetings, as we have observed them, is somewhat different. They often resemble conventional local government meetings, being dominated by the presentation of reports. While it is clearly important to provide information of this sort to forum members, whose day-to-day involvement is necessarily limited, communication tends to be largely one-way, with little time for open discussion or the introduction of new issues. Strategic as well as operational matters in fact are frequently dealt with elsewhere, often at executive board level, with the result that the EAF is reduced to performing a rubber-stamping and report-receiving role rather then a deliberative one.

Parents and other community representatives who lack access to formal and informal networks are particularly disadvantaged in such a situation, leading to a concern that EAFs sometimes serve as an exercise in impression management rather than as a vehicle for frank and open debate of the direction being taken by the zone. There are also concerns that the membership of forums is not representative of the constituencies that EAZs are designed to empower. Although not only a problem for EAZs, community involvement (other than from local businesses) is often limited, and the majority of forum members tend to be white and in professional or managerial occupations (Dickson *et al.*, 2001). Moroever, the relatively high level of involvement in forum discussions by the business partners and headteacher members far outweighs that of the community representatives, including parents, whose contributions are minimal, a finding which replicates what is known of the workings of school governing bodies under LMS.

Finally, the participating schools that send representatives to the forum, which more often than not are headteachers, and only rarely classroom teachers, do not do so on the basis of having ceded any of their existing powers of governance to the zone. The result is that if a zone school does not like the strategic approach which the overwhelming majority of forum members wish to put in place, it can opt out and go its own way. In other words, schools participating in an education action zone are under no obligation to adopt policies it puts forward, even when these articulate fully with a previously agreed action plan and with what most other schools want.

It could be argued that these findings are not typical of every EAZ, of which, after all, there are over seventy operating. On the other hand, our findings connect fully with what is known about those complementary school governance practices that followed the introduction of the local management of schools. In any event, getting people more involved in collective decision-making about local policy for schools is not easy to achieve at the best of times. Indeed, a recent review to which I contributed of current initiatives in this area, both in this country and elsewhere in the world (see Whitty *et al.*, 1998, ch. 7), throws into sharp relief the problems that reforms of this kind encounter, not all of which are straightforwardly a consequence of weaknesses in the policies themselves. Often they reflect some of the long-standing difficulties of implicating people in local decision-making, particularly when they have felt pushed to the margins of the democratic process in the past.

However, some of the practices underway in the two zones we observed do not appear to operate in ways likely to encourage greater democratic involvement. This issue has particular significance given the important symbolic role EAFs are designed to play in legitimating EAZs as local accountability experiments in collective planning for school improvement. In this connection, it seems that EAZ policy may also be creating a new and significant managerial position in the form of the EAZ director. EAZ directors are potentially influential by virtue both of the bureaucratic power invested in their role and the informal power they are able to wield behind the scenes. While formally accountable to EAFs, they appear much less *practically* accountable, either to their individual forums or to the local community they are meant to be serving. To some extent this may be due to external constraints, in particular the speed with which EAZs were implemented. In addition, because EAZs are given priority access to numerous new government initiatives, EAZ directors are under pressure not only to apply for any and all additional funds, but also to spend them within exceedingly tight time frames. Such a situation seems to encourage immediate and unilateral action on a fairly regular basis.

As currently constituted, the EAFs we have observed do not appear to be examples of the kind of 'little polities' about which I wrote so positively earlier. Nor as yet are there many significant signs that the EAZs in question are beginning to provide 'the capability citizens need for the task of regenerating civil society' (Ranson, 2000, p. 263). But, equally, the EAFs we have researched do not seem to be having the kind of dire consequences predicted by some of their worst critics. Certainly, we have uncovered no evidence to suggest that business involvement in EAZ activity is leading to a diminution of the role of other interest groups. If anything, what we discern is a further consolidation of professional and managerial interests, notably that represented by the LEA, zone managers and the headteachers of participating schools.

I want to conclude this section by identifying four aspects of the work of EAFs that could profitably be looked at and improved upon so as to enhance their effectiveness and that of other comparable bodies. First, there is a need to think through in a more explicit way than hitherto the contribution they might make to the revitalization of local democracy. Saccharine discourses that over-emphasize consensual forms of 'partnership', which tend to be the norm, may obscure rather than illuminate what needs to be done here, to the extent that these have a tendency to avoid subjects about which it is difficult to reach agreement – in other words, the very issues that constitute more vital foci for political deliberation about the purposes of education.

Second, there is a need to develop types of forum meeting that encourage greater participation, including the use of opportunities to enable members of the localities within which EAZs are situated to observe and contribute to their proceedings. This is likely to involve encouraging EAFs to reflect more closely in their membership the perspectives of currently underrepresented groups.

Third, there would be value in clarifying better the purpose of the forum in relation to strategic and operational decision-making, alongside the respective decision-making capacities of other zone committees, in particular executive ones. Fourth, it might be worth finding better ways to overcome the 'individualizing' effect of recent reforms such as LMS so that there is more to be gained from working together. At the moment, as I remarked above, schools participate in zones largely on their terms, rather than because of a need to act collectively with others to address a common set of problems. While the implementation of reforms along some of these lines is clearly no guarantee of the policy's success in the future, they may go some way towards addressing some of its current limitations as well as giving hints about how better to create settings in which citizens can democratically debate and determine local education policy.

Of course, there are those reading these suggestions who might argue that *any* mode of devolved responsibility for education involving citizens in helping to make local policy for school provision is bound to fail because people generally are simply not up to taking advantage of it, and indeed would make things worse rather than better. This is a familiar argument. Raymond Williams however put it to flight a long time ago, and his words, which are always worth repeating in contexts such as this, are as follows:

> I have . . . been told, repeatedly, that people are just not interested enough – even, behind the hand, not intelligent enough – to make these new [democratic] institutions and processes work. The usual evidence offered is the cynicism and apathy surrounding existing electoral and democratic forms. None of us can ignore this, yet equally none of us can know how much of it is the predictable consequence of merely apparent involvement in decision-making. Too many familiar processes frustrate or default on actual decisions, or somehow lose them in the carefully protected intricacies of reference elsewhere, that anyone can feel discouraged. But it would be absurd to reject new principles and practices on the

evidence of the very faults of those whose older principles and practices which now make changes necessary. In truth nobody can
know how any of it would work until some of it has been tried.
And it has certainly not, in any general way, been tried.

(1983, p. 104)

Summary

In this chapter I have argued that the promotion of greater equality of
opportunity in and access to education requires new, utopian-like
modes of school governance that are profoundly and differently democratic from the ones currently in place. Thus, rather than being overly
preoccupied with defending the need to maintain some kind of democratic *control* of education, which is more the norm in discussions of
these sorts of things, this chapter has been concerned to provoke
consideration of new ways to increase democratic *involvement* in the
running of schools via actions that promote inclusiveness, participation
and dialogue. These actions include reinventing what counts as legiti-
mate public gatherings and encouraging alternative ways of debating
and making decisions within them. In Chapter 7 we will look at the
implications of some of this for what schools should teach and the
nature of the pupil learning experience they ought to provide.

7 A utopian cultural core curriculum

We are not concerned with showing that any particular subject is to be taught for reasons intrinsic to the subject. . . . Think more about the pupils and less about the internal logic . . . of your subjects.

(The Content of Education: Proposals for the Reform of the School Curriculum (1945))

Education in *Utopia*

In More's Utopia, schooling is universally available, offering a 'modern' kind of education. By 'modern', I mean that for the sixteenth century, it is an up-to-the-minute and ahead-of-its time-education. It is also a distinctively radical and innovative, providing opportunities to learn that go well beyond the 'basics', embracing personal and social development and openings to pursue extra-curricular activities.

But, what of the twenty-first century? What kind of 'modern' curriculum best suits its school-age pupils? And what kind of utopian thought experiment might we conduct to answer such a question? In Chapter 3, I suggested that such an experiment might start out from our asking: 'What would the school curriculum look like if its subject matter were chosen largely in terms of its contribution to helping children to live a full life rather than in relation to the short-term needs of the economy?' In this chapter I propose, like Tom Bentley in Chapter 4, to answer this question, albeit in a more roundabout way than he does, by first asking and addressing two further questions: What kind of society should schools today be helping pupils to live a 'full life' within?; and What dispositions and ways of knowing will enable them to live successfully and contribute fully to such a life? In seeking to answer the second of these questions, I will draw upon my own utopian imagination to relativize the current preoccupation schools have with subject-based curricula in order to propose a quite different way of thinking of the form and content of compulsory education. In addressing the first question, I will excavate the analyses of a number of prominent contemporary social theorists.

The social revolutions of our time

Chapter 4 offered a brief analysis of the nature of modern society, in particular the most significant social revolutions presently underway within it which are radically reconfiguring how life is currently experienced and lived, and which I now want to insist demand a fresh curricular response from schools.

Following Giddens (1994), these revolutions arise out of and are constituted by four very significant and all-engulfing societal processes: the influence of intensifying *globalization*; the expansion of *social reflexivity* and *individualization*; the emergence of a *post-traditional* social order; and the increased sense of living in an *uncertain, precarious, risk-satiated* world.

Globalization is ordinarily understood in purely economic terms. More often than not, it is used to draw attention to the manner in which commercial activities, fuelled by advances in instantaneous electronic communication, now span and integrate fiscally the capitalist/developed world in dramatically new ways. But this is only part of the matter. For while globalization is, for sure, an economic, 'out-there' phenomenon, it is also a social and ultimately personal 'in-here' one too. As Giddens (1994, pp. 4–5) observes:

> Globalization does not only concern the creation of large-scale systems, but also the transformation of local, and even personal, contexts of social experience. Our day-to-day activities are increasingly influenced by events happening on the other side of the world. Conversely, local lifestyle habits have become globally consequential. Thus my decision to buy a certain item of clothing has implications not only for the international division of labour but for the earth's ecosystems.

Globalization, then, is to do with more than worldwide twenty-four-hour money markets; it is also about the transforming of some of our basic institutions and the manner too in which we personally experience time and space, entailing radical shifts in our conceptions of duration and proximity, the latter of which cause us to question the sense we have of our local, national and international cultural identities. This unraveling process articulates with a simultaneous rise in new modes of individualism, the backdrop to which includes the emergence of a post-traditional perspective on how we should live our lives, which is infused by a heightened form of social reflexivity and insecurity.

These new modes individualism, it needs to be stressed immediately, denote neither market individualism nor the atomization of social experience, but rather the variety of ways in which people are now 'invited to constitute themselves as individuals: to plan, understand, and design themselves as individuals' (Beck, quoted in Giddens, 1998, p. 36). There is, in fact, a sense in which we are all today routinely caught up in 'everyday experiments' (Giddens, 1994, p. 93) involving 'a multiplicity of changes and adaptations in daily life . . . deciding "how to be" in respect of the body . . . what one's "sexuality" is, as well as grasp what "relationships" are and how they might best be constructed' (1994, pp. 82–3), and which therefore require us to choose among alternatives. Put another way, the modern social order is one characterized by constant and ubiquitous change, but with no clear direction of development or response.

Certainly, within a host of key sites of social practice, everyday life is taking fresh and, in some cases, potentially unsettling directions. Within the site of economic production, for example, the speeding up of turnover time arising out of new modes of capital accumulation, including flexibility in the labour market, is accompanied by parallel accelerations in exchange and consumption which accentuate volatility and ephemerality of fashions, products and production techniques. Within the family, and intimate relations generally, the emergence of 'pure' or 'convenience relationships' (Giddens, 1991, pp. 87–98), which are 'sought only for what [they] . . . can bring to the partners involved', and a form of decentred sexuality freed 'from the needs of reproduction' (Giddens, 1992, pp. 2 and 27) are placing new demands on people who previously looked to religion or mainstream morality for guidance about how best to construct and live their personal lives. Such 'traditions', as was stressed in Chapter 1, no longer hold sway in the way they did once, for (to repeat what I wrote there, requoting Giddens) 'tradition [today] must more and more be contemplated, defended, sifted through, in relation to the awareness that there exists a variety of ways of doing things' (1994, p. 83).

In following this process through, individuals are confronted not only by a variety of ways of doing things, but by a host of uncertainties about what counts as the 'correct' way of doing them. Coupled with a sense of the precariousness of things generally, or what some sociologists refer to as living in a 'risk society', people today are forced to accommodate and develop responses to a range of what Giddens

(1994) calls 'manufactured [human-made] uncertainties', the most significant of which include global warming, international terrorism, meat infectivity, HIV/Aids and GM crops. Some people's responses to such uncertainties take the form of denial or neglect; for others, they entail strategic lifestyle adjustments and new modes of political involvement and civic engagement generally. Either way, the fragility of modern living creates dilemmas which everyone is constrained to confront, one way or another. To that extent, active risk-taking and the management of risk are chronically inscribed elements of modern social living – elements with which, in order to live a meaningful life, we all need to learn to cope better, and for which pupils in schools arguably need to be well prepared.

Another element is the search for a personal identity that makes sense as we all seek to come to terms with and live purposively within a modern society that is more complex, differentiated and pluralistic than any other in human history. Indeed, it is because such a society does not allow for the luxury of having unified, least of all singular, identities that we are all faced with the challenge today of how to construct personal, differentiated ones that enable us to live in a morally coherent and consistent way. For schooling, a key issue thus becomes how to introduce new curricula that assist pupils better to develop (as Quicke observes) their capacities to 'evaluate expertise and think rationally about appropriate courses of action in conditions of risk and uncertainty' (1999, p. 11). Indeed, a central dilemma facing contemporary schooling within modern societies is how best to foster among pupils the necessary skills and dispositions that stretch their capabilities in ways that help them to make more of themselves than is immediately apparent, and which in turn nurture in them the hope that what they do with their lives matters and makes sense.

Central to this project is the need to encourage in pupils a commitment to a form of creative lifelong learning – 'creative' because it helps them to think and act imaginatively as they come to terms with the 'risk society' within which they are compelled to live; 'lifelong' because it is not restricted to any one point or phase in their lives.

Learning and self-creation

Like 'choice' in education, 'learning' is something of which everyone approves. On the other hand, like choice, learning is difficult to define with precision. We all recognize its importance; but what we are less clear about is what it actually means and denotes. Much the same may be said about 'lifelong learning'. On quick reflection it seems to be an easy idea to understand. But further thought reveals otherwise. For a start, there are competing models of lifelong learning, including contrasting conceptions of how it should be provided (Elliott, 2001; Field, 2002; Longworth and Davies, 1996). Attempting definitions in this area is therefore a risky business.

My own understanding of these issues leads me to conclude that learning is best appreciated if it is seen as a *process of discovery* that generates in people new understandings about themselves and the world around them (Seltzer and Bentley, 1999; Watkins *et al.*, 2002). Because it is a process of discovery, learning offers all of us an increased capacity for self-creation. To that extent, it is a form of becoming. Accordingly, one way of defining what is meant by 'lifelong learning' is to think of it as the means whereby an individual develops comprehensively and creatively throughout her or his lifetime.

While this must entail, of course, the need to increase people's access to institutions and expand their opportunities to learn generally, new avenues of this kind are only part of the story. The full narrative needs, in addition, to include something about the sorts of conditions that are likely to foster the kind of creative learning which helps school-age children to navigate successfully their current and future lives, something about which I will write more below.

Creative learners

Before that, I want briefly to identify what I consider are the key qualities possessed by creative learners – qualities that need to be encouraged within schools in order to enable pupils to embrace a lifelong commitment to learning.

According to Seltzer and Bentley (1999, pp. 26–9), creative learners have four key qualities. First, they are extremely open to new ideas and new situations. As such, they are people who allow, indeed encourage, their presuppositions about themselves and the world to be challenged by others. Creative learners are thus post-traditional learners, for they recognize that there are likely to be a variety of ways of acting in a particular situation, rather than the one or two preferred options dictated by past precedent.

Second, creative learners are people who have the ability to transfer knowledge acquired in one context to another to solve problems. As such, they are adaptable people who do not ultimately depend on others to either define or solve problems for them.

Third, creative learners are people who recognize that learning does not always come easily, but are sufficiently internally motivated to seek out innovative ways to overcome the difficulties this poses. On this understanding, creative learners discern a purpose in learning that helps them to be predisposed hopefully to the problems that life throws up. To that extent, creative learners are better equipped than their uncreative counterparts to live imaginatively without certainty.

Fourth, creative learners, because they are motivated learners, are often tenacious in their approach to the resolution of problems. They take it for granted that learning is an incremental process often requiring repeated effort for it to lead to success. The tenacious creative learner is thus someone who is not put off easily by initial failure or distracted by superficial quick-fix solutions to problems.

Becoming a lifelong learner is thus centrally about acquiring the characteristics of the creative learner, as I have defined them. Indeed, lifelong learning is constituted by the very creative process I have described above. Thus lifelong learners are open-minded, adaptable, highly motivated individuals who have the confidence to focus attention in the pursuit of a goal, and to do so repeatedly as circumstances require.

But how can the creative learning that constitutes lifelong learning be encouraged within schools, and what are some of the school-specific barriers that frustrate its achievement?

Security and creative learning

Let me begin to answer this question with one further general observation about creative learning – which is to do with the fact that its encouragement depends crucially on the availability of learning environments within which pupils feel safe and secure in terms of being able to take risks and to learn from failure.

In mentioning 'safety' and 'security' at this point, what I am trying to convey is something of their psychic relevance to understanding better the nature of the learning process. My source of inspiration at this point is partly Seltzer and Bentley (1999), but chiefly Freud, who over seventy years ago argued in *Civilization and its Discontents* that the chief gift 'civilization' brings to people is *security* – security from the many 'dangers' which he considered came from nature, one's own body and other people. While Freud's definition of 'danger' here is highly questionable, and completely irrelevant to the concerns of this book, his use of the term 'security' is most certainly not.

The German translation of the English word 'security' is *sicherheit*. This word manages to squeeze into a single term complex phenomena for which the English language needs at least three terms to convey –

'security' being one, and 'certainty' and 'safety' being the other two. According to Freud, all three ingredients of *sicherheit* are conditions of self-confidence and self-reliance, on which the ability to think and act creatively depend. The absence, or near absence, of any of the three ingredients has much the same effect – the dissipation of self-assurance and the loss of trust in one's own ability, followed in quick succession by anxiety and growing incapacitation.

If Freud is right here, we need to ask ourselves how far the kinds of learning environment we provide in schools lead to a sense of *sicherheit* among the pupils who study in them. I suspect that, too often, many do not, particularly when these encourage and are based upon a competitive ethos.

Competition and creativity

While competitive environments within the economic sphere undoubtedly foster creative product design, their use in educational contexts concerned to promote creative learning is questionable. Competitive environments, notably ones that result in hierarchies of esteem within and between schools, by definition, produce winners and losers. The fostering of creative forms of lifelong learning cannot surely be premised on the idea that one can lose out in any learning environment or get a second-rate education in another.

While a certain amount of failure is inevitable and necessary for the creative learning process, being a 'loser' in school or within a system of schooling cannot be. Rather, what is needed are new opportunities in schools for pupils to feel confident enough to take risks and learn from failure instead of being branded by it. From the pupils' perspective, it is a matter (as Seltzer and Bentley assert) of them feeling able to react positively to self-help questions like: 'Am I safe here?' 'Do I belong?' 'Can I count on others to support me?' 'Should I stay?' Indeed, the challenge here is for schools to foster 'a sense of comfort and positive expectancy', so that their pupils feel ready to take part fully in the learning process (1999, pp. 31–2).

Recognizing difference

This value of self-confidence is especially important for those pupils from economically less well-off backgrounds who have been over many years disadvantaged by education, indeed often been 'failed' by it. The challenge here is not simply about finding better ways of redistributing resources in ways that favour such pupils – though that, of course, is part of it – but how to generate that more compre-hensive understanding that validates their worth irrespective of back-ground.

One practical means of delivering on this objective is to increase the range of opportunities for all pupils to have some say in the form, content and pace of their own learning. Indeed, there is some evidence to suggest that, once pupils learn to trust the learning environment, they develop a strong desire to exercise greater control over the direction of the learning that takes place within it. Encouraging ownership in this way is important as a vital means of developing greater autonomy and responsibility among pupils, two of the hallmarks of the creative learner to which I alluded earlier.

To that extent, teachers may need to rethink further the nature of their pedagogic role in school which, on this understanding, indicates the importance of shifting away from a teaching approach to a learning one (Watkins *et al.*, 2002). A central feature of this shift in emphasis must be the promotion of highly active modes of learning that engage pupils' interests, discourage passivity and demote didactic teaching approaches. Teaching is much more than telling, and learning is definitely much more than listening. Thus, contrary to current UK government thinking on these matters, my view is that we need less whole-class teaching (for which read 'instruction') in our schools. Instead, schools need to find more imaginative ways of developing problem-solving approaches to the learning of new subject matter, including those that entail a strong element of independent investigation.

Creativity and the subject curriculum

All of this, of course, is again easier written down than actually done, particularly in today's school settings where so much emphasis is placed upon 'delivering' a prescribed, subject-based curriculum and meeting externally determined and monitored performance targets. The audit culture, which so many teachers are now required to follow, is in many ways antithetical to the creative learning process I have described, not to mention the philosophy of lifelong learning to which I have linked it. To be sure, regulatory control over the nature of the UK's National Curriculum has undergone considerable amend-ment in recent times, with the result that schools in England now have more discretion over what should be taught. On the other hand, the basic unit around which learning in most British schools is struc-tured remains the lesson: one lesson, usually – in the secondary phase, certainly – in the course of which one subject is taught to one class.

While this is clearly an economically efficient way of organizing pupil learning, in the sense that it enables resources to be co-ordinated and distributed effectively, we need to ask if it helps to develop the sort of creative learning approach to which I referred above, in particular the emphasis it places upon the importance of being able to transfer knowledge acquired in one context to another in order to solve problems. My own view is that it hinders rather than helps this process, to the extent that a subject-based curriculum taught in relatively isolated bits and parts is more likely to be an inflexible curriculum that contributes to an unnecessary fragmentation of the learning experience.

A school curriculum concerned to promote creative learning and a commitment to learning throughout life must surely be organized along quite different lines, and with quite different purposes in mind. If there is a need for separate specialist courses – and I can easily concede that there might be from time to time – these should always be perceived as relating to and illuminating others of a more general nature. What matters is not the coherence in curriculum organization that is the product of imaginative timetabling within schools, but coherence in the learning experience of pupils – the degree, that is, to which the curriculum makes sense to them rather than to their teachers.

One way of releasing the stranglehold of the subject curriculum on our thinking about the nature of creative learning is to be reminded of what are actually school subjects. As everyone knows, school subjects derive their names and value from the academic disciplines – the subjects cultivated in universities and other seats of high learning. What is less well known is the extent to which the academic disciplines within these contexts are not fixed fields of enquiry with visible boundaries. On the contrary, within higher education, any one discipline may contain contested – even contradictory – points of view. Moreover, whatever a university discipline has accumulated in the way of literature, criticism, theories and so on over the years is being exposed continuously by the members of its academic community to re-evaluation and reinterpretation, a process influenced by shifts of emphasis within contemporary society as well as by developments within the discipline itself.

To that extent, the subject curriculum found in the majority of British schools, and prescribed by the UK's National Curriculum, is both a sham representation of and narrow selection from the host of disciplines of knowledge found within the curricula of universities –

a sham representation because it does not reflect accurately the intellectual dynamism of those disciplines; a narrow selection because it leaves out of consideration a variety of arguably key ways in which universities engage in disciplined enquiry, such as is found in their departments of philosophy, sociology, politics, psychology, to mention only a few. Neither observation however prevents school subjects from being regarded by their advocates as authoritative bodies of knowledge that are capable of being passed on to pupils, bit by bit, through the medium of individual lessons. This myth not only legitimizes the UK National Curriculum specification, it also sanctions the efforts of time-tablers to reproduce it locally within particular schools.

As I see it, the problem we face in seeking to foster creative learning of the kind I have described is not one about how best to timetable and teach the prestructured and prescribed subject matter of a particular subject or set of subjects, but rather to devise situations in which pupils are led to create for themselves sustained structures of thinking and meaning around well-chosen subject matter – a case, in other words, of seeing school subjects as resources in the construction of the curriculum, rather than determinants of its overall structure and emphasis.

Progressive discourses about the creative learning process in schools, if they are to exert the maximum influence, thus need to be hitched up to equally imaginative design solutions to the problem of what subject matter pupils should be exposed to. Put this way, school learning theorists, many of whom proffer challenging understandings of the variety of ways in which children learn, including the best ways to promote learning in general and for specific purposes, cannot sensibly duck the question of what should be learned and what kind of learning outcomes are more or less useful to pupils in navigating their current and future personal and social lives. Thus conceived, *pedagogy and curriculum are best viewed as two sides of the same coin*. But, equally, developing the sorts of imaginative design solutions about the content and products of learning entails thinking anew the guiding principles and conceptualizations that govern the way in which school curricula are presently constructed.

In the remaining sections of this chapter I intend therefore to outline a utopian vision of what these principles and organizing ideas might look like, including the broad outline of the sort of curriculum they might give rise to if applied in practice. This will entail my being mildly nostalgic – an aspect of the utopian imagination I strongly spoke up for in Chapter 2 – inasmuch as I will seek to restore to public attention and sympathy a somewhat lapsed theoretical, prescriptive and radical way of thinking about the content of a reformed compulsory 'core' curriculum of general education.

While the approach I will commend was a very prominent feature of curriculum theorizing some twenty or more years ago, notably within certain UK university departments of education, it became obscured and ultimately overtaken in the 1990s by conceptions of national curriculum policy-making which fell back upon historically sanctified subject-based notions of what schools should teach. My view is that this earlier approach was ahead of its time, and that only now can its full relevance and significance be fully appreciated, chiefly because its understanding of modern society and the purposes of school education resonate better with how people now experience and think about their lives than was the case then.

The launching pad for this approach is a particular conception of culture and its relationship to society and education; and its point of departure is the suggestion that schools should become key sites for cultural renewal instead of vessels for the dissemination of subject knowledge.

Culture and the curriculum

It was once intellectually fashionable to describe the content of education as either a selection from or a representation of culture. Denis Lawton, for example, some twenty-seven years ago, argued that when we think about any school curriculum we are affirming a view of the living culture of society (1975, pp. 5–7). Writing at about the same time, Malcolm Skilbeck developed this insight, likening the school curriculum to a 'map of culture' (1976, pp. 83–7), by which he meant some kind of representation of the main features and tendencies of the contemporary world. Anticipating both of these suggestions, Raymond Williams observed in the 1960s that the content of education is best understood as an expression of 'certain basic elements in the culture . . . a particular set of emphases and omissions' (1961, p. 145), and that a reformed system of schooling should provide opportunities for pupils to engage in active debate and amendment of what this comprises.

However, if one accepts the general principle that much of what is to be taught in schools can be decided by reference to cultural rather than subject considerations, a great deal still hinges on the concept of culture that is taken to be educationally relevant. To begin with there is the familiar distinction between two conceptions of culture: the descriptive, anthropological characterization of culture as 'a whole way of life', and the normative or evaluative conception representing 'the best that has been thought and said'. Thus, when people talk of basing the content of education on the culture of society, they may be either suggesting that schools should be centrally concerned with socializing their pupils in particular ways, or encouraging us to discuss the curriculum in terms of what are considered to be the most valued aspects of the intellectual and aesthetic achievements of society, sometimes called its 'cultural heritage'. A leaning in curriculum design towards the former interpretation of culture is likely to lead to a somewhat conservative and limited conception of the purposes of education; embracing the latter notion of culture, on the other hand, may foster a view of there being two or more cultures – specifically, high and low, or elite and mass cultures – the adoption of either of which can have serious and potentially negative implications for curriculum planning and the practice of education generally.

To escape the curriculum limitations of these notions of culture, while seeking to hang on to the way in which each encourages an appreciation of the content of education that is not restricted to the teaching of subjects, we need to identify a different way of thinking culturally about the school curriculum which shifts our understanding beyond notions of cultural assimilation and cultural elitism.

Culture as a structuring process

The social theorist Zygmunt Bauman is a useful source at this point. In his (1973) book *Culture as Praxis,* Bauman distinguishes three co-existing concepts of culture: the hierarchical, the differential and the generic. 'Hierarchical' conceptions of culture feature strongly in the account offered above, in which reference is made to 'high' and 'low' graduations of cultural engagement; 'differential' conceptions of culture were also to the fore in the same analysis, specifically in the suggestion that the essential features of any society are capable of being discerned through cataloging its characteristic customs, beliefs, laws, capabilities and relations.

The 'generic' concept of culture, by contrast, has neither an evaluative nor a descriptive dimension, denoting instead the *process* through which the members of any society construct systems of meaning that enable them to make sense of and engage purposively with their life-worlds. On this understanding, 'culture' is not so much a possession or detachable feature of society, but instead a *signifying process* through which its members interact in communication in their various specific relationships and social practices generally.

This way of thinking about 'culture' encourages us to think of 'society' as being more than just an aggregate of individuals and groups, pointing up instead the extent to which it is the sum of the relations within which such individuals and groups stand. Thus a society has whatever distinctive form and content it has by virtue of the fact that it is 'held together' by a particular 'structure of being and feeling' (its culture), which is constituted by the relations between the kinds of practices that make it up. A prerequisite of people being related in this way is their membership of a common culture that furnishes them with the necessary concepts which constitute both the means whereby their social practices are carried on, and the way they are carried on. Accordingly, 'society', including its 'risk' and 'post-traditional' variants, is best thought of as a cultural assemblage of institutionalized social practices or patterns of relationships reproduced across time and space.

Giddens refers to this process as the 'duality of structure', an expression created by him to draw attention to the essential recursiveness of social life whereby 'society' is both the ever-present condition and the continually reproduced product of human agency: 'structure is both medium and outcome of the reproduction of practices. Structure enters simultaneously into the constitution of the agent and social practice, and "exists" in the generating moments of this constitution' (1979, p. 5). To that extent, 'culture', conceived as 'structure', forms both personality and society simultaneously.

Sites of social practice and the core curriculum

If 'society' is not to be viewed as an aggregate of separable events and individuals and groups, but rather as a 'structured' and causally efficacious whole that is being continually reproduced and transformed as a result of people's active participation in a common culture, how are we to distinguish aspects of this complexus for the purposes of curriculum planning? Or, to put this another way, if 'culture' is to be understood as a noun of process, rather than as a hierarchical or differential term, how might it helpfully guide our thinking about the character of a reformed core curriculum?

To answer these questions, I propose to identify and briefly describe the various stages in the process of planning such a curriculum. These all start out from a crucial acknowledgement: that curriculum planning of this sort inescapably entails taking seriously the proposition that determining the content of education requires a form of what Skilbeck calls 'cultural mapping', in the course of which particular social practices, or features of the common culture of society, are identified as foundational, and thus warranting critical exploration and transformation within the programmes of study offered by schools.

In my schema, this acknowledgement is followed quickly by the proposition that we should distinguish for curriculum planning purposes those major sites of social practice that are regarded as characteristic of advanced capitalist social formations, of which of course the UK is a typical example, and which are currently undergoing significant change and reconstitution.

I want to suggest that there are three such sites: the site of production; the site of the state; and the site of the family. The site of capitalist production is characterized by private property in the means of market exchange, wage labour and investment, each of which is being transformed radically under the influence of globalized economic activity; the state by the institutions of liberal democracy, which are also having to manage increasingly borderless economies as well as react positively to the demise of conventional party political behaviour; and the family by the structure of power and kinship known as patriarchy, which is significantly under threat from the rise of 'convenience' relationships and the growing economic independence of women.

These three sites are foundational to the extent that they define the three major relations which ultimately reproduce individuals within capitalist society and which simultaneously reproduce capitalist society itself, with all its attendant risks and uncertainties. Each person has, at the same time, a specific citizenship, gender and class location, though their articulation often occasions a number of contradictory or inconsistent effects. For instance, while the state is organized according to the principle of majority rule, production is structured in such a way as to maintain working people in a largely subordinate role. Similarly, recent structural amendments to the status of women in the family and the economy do not overly extend to the institutions of liberal democracy within which they still remain under-represented.

The next stage in the planning process requires us to single out for educational purposes those social practices considered to be integral to each site, and any other sub-site considered to be significant, and on that basis to develop curricula that include schemes of work which enable pupils to develop the necessary creative dispositions and competencies to navigate successfully their way through them in a manner that is immediately purposive and ultimately meaningful. While these schemes would highlight for investigation aspects of social practice, rather than bits of subjects, this does not entail the denial of disciplined enquiry, but rather its deployment for the purposes of cultural renewal, the subject-matter of which would also draw on other less formalized patterns of meaning such as are found in norms of conduct and other common value and social expectations. These schemes would moreover engage directly with the kinds of uncertainties and life choice issues to which I drew attention in my earlier discussion of the social revolutions of our time – in particular those involving 'how to be', 'behave' and 'become' in a modern risky social order. As such, they would add up to a genuinely 'modern' curriculum in the sense that, together, they embrace the imperatives of new individualism and the tenets of the post-traditional outlook.

Using the school curriculum as a vehicle for interrogating and seeking to transform those social practices considered integral to the sites of cultural practice I have identified has important implications for the nature of teaching and learning. If the primary purpose of studies in the core curriculum is to assist pupils to become active interpreters of culture, they will need to include opportunities for them to learn the knowledge and to practise the skills most closely associated with each site. Thus political awareness and an understanding of fundamental economic categories, each reinforced by active involvement in one or more related practical exercises, would seem to be a necessary minimum.

Other specifics excepted, the aim throughout is to increase pupils' discursive understanding and penetration of the social systems to whose constitution they and the rest of us contribute – that is, to enhance their structuring capabilities as these affect distinctive forms of social practice. The means to this end are common learning situations and processes that foster those critical and creative dispositions from which new cultural and social possibilities can emerge.

Figure 7.1 captures pictorially what this version of the core curriculum might look like in practice. It would be idle to pretend that this portrait offers more than an indicative guide to the selection of curriculum content and how learning should be approached. As a guide, however, it does pinpoint the need for schools to consider how subjects may be used as resources in, rather than the starting point of, curriculum construction. It also challenges conceptions of teaching and learning in schools that fail to give sufficiently high priority to pupil-directed enquiry and analysis and criticism – active engagement with materials, persons and ideas, in other words. For, in the absence of such a spirit of criticality, pupils can hardly be expected to take an active part in appraising and reinterpreting the range of social practices which they would be invited to confront in the core curriculum and in their lives generally.

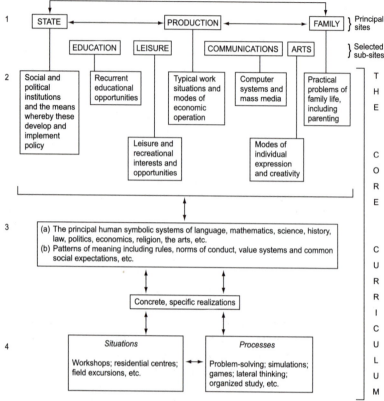

Figure 7.1 An alternative way of conceptualizing a common core curriculum.
Source: Reynolds and Skilbeck, 1976, p. 124.

Summary

Every human society has its own shape, purposes and meanings or culture. Indeed, the making of society – reproducing and transforming it – is centrally to do with looking for and identifying common meanings and directions through active debate and amendment. Education, and schooling in particular, has a crucial part to play in this critical process, particularly at this point in time when society is undergoing such radical and rapid change, much of the direction of which is difficult to predict with certainty, and when the construction of personal identities that make sense to their owners is a more problematic project than at any other moment in human history. Accordingly, thinking through the implications of all this for the design of school curricula, including the forms of learning they should promote, is both a necessary and inevitably utopian exercise.

This chapter has worked at this exercise in a variety of ways. It first identified a range of major shifts in consciousness underway in modern society, prompted respectively by intensifying globalization, the expansion of social reflexivity, the emergence of a post-traditional social order, and the increased sense of living in a risk-satiated world, to which it was argued a curricular response is urgently required. It then outlined a conception of creative lifelong learning as a necessary means to address successfully the challenges posed by these shifts, which was then associated with a form of school curriculum provision that gives priority to cultural renewal rather than the teaching of subjects.

The intention throughout has been to relativize the subject curriculum in order to foreground more relevant and more inclusive programmes of study for school pupils that offer them the opportunity to develop those creative, inventive and critical capacities most likely to assist them to achieve personal and contribute to social change. The final chapter, Chapter 8, will translate this vision into a set of maxims for putting the hope back into education in general and into the practice of teaching in particular.

8   Putting hope back into education

The situation is hopeless, and the solution hopelessly simple.

(Paul Watzlawick)

Pandora's Box

In Greek mythology – in one version of the story – the gods give Pandora a sealed jar containing all the evils of the world, plus one good, Hope, which is compressed at the bottom. Curious about what the jar contains, Pandora opens it, causing all the sorrows, diseases, quarrels and woes that have ever since afflicted human beings to fly out. Realizing what she has done, Pandora hastily snaps back the lid of the jar, but she is too late to prevent the plague of evils from escaping into the world. Only Hope, which is slower than the rest, remains trapped inside.

In this short final chapter, I want to suggest some 'signposts' to ways in which hope might be released out of education's Pandora's Box so as to foster a revitalized sense of optimism and pro-activity among those schoolteachers whose resolve about the job in hand is currently lower than they would wish it to be, and whose sense of vocation is being sorely tested as a result. I am referring again at this point to teachers such as the one who featured strongly in Chapter 1, whose mournful words – 'I'm not sure I have much hope or faith left' – echo throughout much of what I have written thus far.

The occasion of writing this chapter also provides an opportunity to draw together for a directly practical purpose some of the more significant strands of abstract analysis that have made up much of the book's discussion. Having written a book about hope in education, I ought to have something encouraging to say to teachers whose sense of being hopeful about their work is presently much reduced. Accordingly, I will reiterate and integrate some of the themes introduced in early chapters, with the aim of prompting among such teachers a renewed sense of the importance of the work that they do, as well as a fresh commitment to the manner in which they go about it.

By writing in this way, I need speedily to stress, there is no suggestion of offering teachers ready-made solutions to the depressive work experiences many of them are forced each day to endure, some of which, in any event, are not within their control or even influence. This applies particularly to those aspects of their work circumstances that reflect inadequacies in funding and resources generally. In addition, the poor motivation evident in some pupils' commitment to schooling is not always within teachers' power to influence for the better, however hard they try. On the other hand, being faced with such difficulties still requires some personal response or coping strategy on their part. For a small minority, this undoubtedly amounts to a mixture of cynical resignation and apathetic inactivity. For the rest – the majority – it entails a fearsome unwillingness to be borne down by negative circumstances, allied to a conviction to overcome them.

The three positive general signposts towards putting the hope back into education which I will write about in this chapter are written with that majority group of teachers in mind, and especially for those among them whose confidence is being eroded by the hard daily effort of trying. To that extent, this chapter is about supporting their efforts, written in the spirit of recognizing that without them the situation in our schools would be a whole lot worse. For this book is targeted at teachers who are fundamentally optimists of the will; who appreciate the extent to which being a teacher is the ultimate in hope; but who feel dispirited by the fact that they cannot do their best for the children for whose learning they are responsible.

Positive signpost 1: Take hopelessness seriously

One interpretation of the teacher's essay which begins Chapter 1 might lead to the conclusion that its author is a shocking complainer, entirely incapable of looking on the bright side of anything in his work. Another, more positive appreciation of what the teacher says is to read his essay as a stirring appeal to make good a situation that he considers to be in terminal decline, and which ought not to be. Thus, to recall the theme of utopian realism from Chapter 4, which I drew upon to highlight the degree to which the seeds of change are often implied in current developments, this teacher is already helping to put hope back into his work by virtue of the fact that he has a submerged vision of what it should be like. Lurking behind his professional narrative of decline, in other words, is the broad outline of a utopia about teaching and learning; and about how schools should be run and managed.

He and I have much in common, therefore, to the extent that we are each troubled by what we see as gross limitations in the current education context – in my case about how schools are governed and managed, and about the kind of curricula they offer; in his, about the motivation and behaviour of the pupils whom he teaches and the state of the buildings in which he works. But because we come from different worlds within education – mine the world of academia; his the world of classroom practice – we differ in the degree to which our personal troubles about education lead each of us to identify and discuss public issues of education policy that might contribute to improvement.

Typically, because I am an academic removed from the hurly-burly of the school classroom, I move quickly from being troubled to thinking analytically. Typically, because the teacher is directly confronted by the subject matter of his troubles, he eschews such intellectualism in favour of being angry about his work context, which speedily translates into blaming other people for the situation within which he finds himself – the pupils, his school managers, the Education Secretary and other politicians.

These aspersions of blame, of course, may be entirely justified; but they must surely represent the launching pad for the teacher partly to make things better himself, or to suggest ways in which they might be made better, rather than be viewed by him as exhausting all avenues of response. To be fair, the teacher does propose some remedial actions, affecting changes in the behaviour of his managers and education's political leaders, but there is not much of even a hint about what he will do differently. To that extent, the teacher is in danger of being far too reactive against others at the expense of any suggestion of personal pro-activity.

The danger of criticism without construction – which is what we have here – is that it leaves everything as it is, and thus compounds the original problem instead of contributing to its resolution. On the other hand, construction without criticism is likely to realize very little of consequence. Accordingly, we should always welcome the latter, if only as a trigger to promote consideration of the former. Moreover, a carefully calibrated criticism that arises out of a state of hopelessness may, paradoxically, liberate those who experience it to embrace modes of exciting reconstruction that, in other, happier circumstances, might not feature as even remote possibilities. As Ulrich Beck and Elizabeth Beck-Gernsheim (2002, p. 193) remark:

> Hopelessness is not exactly a comfortable foundation. But neither is it as bad as its reputation. If one's efforts are most unlikely to have any prospects, they are also freed of much that is tied up and endangered by efforts which can barely stir themselves when the prospects are good. . . . Hopelessness [on this basis] punctures vanity. But, if the hopelessness is finely measured, even the reservations that make thought small and subservient can be broken down. . . . [Thus], in this sense, hopelessness [may be] . . . encouraging. . . . [For] it is [always] possible to start something when [it seems] you have nothing to lose.

A finely measured or an 'educated' negativity, then, may represent a helpful resource for teachers to cope better with the more frustrating vicissitudes of their work, chiefly by providing a means to take some control over events instead of being a victim of them.

Positive signpost 2: Take the moral virtues of teaching seriously

There is an abundance of common-sense evidence to suggest that when people find themselves in dire and difficult circumstances they are also able to sustain themselves by bringing to mind ideas of the good life. Courage, allied to persistence, is often the hallmark of such belligerence in the face of problems that appear intractable. When we see hope seeping out of education, it is important then to remind ourselves that the latter is not only premised on the former, but also that one of the tasks of the progressive educator is to work hard to unveil opportunities for its promotion, no matter what the obstacles may be. For, without hope in the education context, both teachers and pupils lose direction and the capacity to find it. Defeatism in education thus makes no sense, other than as a means of getting by through a surrender to circumstance, a contradiction in terms when one considers those higher order aims of education that emphasize the development of pupils' knowledge and understanding.

Teachers who despair of their work will need therefore partly to help themselves to retain where it is under threat, and to restore when it is has been mislaid, that larger love of teaching that looks for the good in all pupils, a theme which I have linked with the promotion of their dignity. Ultimately, there is no alternative, other than to give up largely or entirely. School managers can assist significantly in this process of retention and renewal, of course, not least by exercising the kinds of invitational leadership roles that were illustrated in the case study in Chapter 5. Easier written down, now as then, than achieved; but what other route is worth following? Fatalism? Cynicism? None of these, as I also argued in Chapter 1, where I suggested that the combination of such responses breeds a useless conservatism, entailing a melancholic false consciousness, that legitimates inactivity instead of providing a coping strategy which makes long-term practical sense.

Positive signpost 3: Take optimistic illusions seriously

One way of fending off such melancholia is to draw on optimistic illusions – or what I have termed elsewhere in this book *vocabularies of hope* – which act as spurs to new action and promote mental well-being generally. Such illusions, however, need to be carefully put together if they are to work the desired effect. If framed too optimistically, they may give rise to foolish risk-taking or 'Walter Mitty-like' behaviour. Thus, while optimistic illusions must be utopian, they need equally to be realistic, and therefore realizable.

On the other hand, teachers should not underestimate the degree to which the adoption of exaggerated perceptions of control and mastery over events can contribute to their ability better to engage in productive and creative work, even in circumstances where this is very difficult. As the psychologist Shelley Taylor (1989) writes: 'Normal human thought and perception is marked not by accuracy, but positive self-enhancing illusions about the self, the world, and the future. Moreover, these illusions appear actually to be adaptive, promoting rather than undermining mental health.' All this connects with my earlier high estimate of the value of utopian daydreaming, which in the education context can encourage the carrying out of thought experiments that assist teachers to recover submerged and positive ways of thinking about their work. This kind of anticipatory consciousness, if conducted publicly and with others, may also provide one of the necessary conditions for initiating collective action for school improvement. It also underscores the importance of keeping to the forefront of one's mind that, however difficult things appear to be, there is likely to be a way of making progress, providing one is prepared to make the effort to find and act upon it. As Raymond Williams (1983, pp. 268–9) once so tellingly remarked:

It is only in a shared belief and insistence that there are practical alternatives that the balance of forces and chances begins to alter. Once the inevitabilities are challenged, we begin gathering our resources for a journey of hope. If there are no easy answers, there are still available and discoverable hard answers, and it is these that we can learn to make and share.

It has been one of the central arguments of this book that such hard answers within education, as well as generally, are capable of being envisaged through exercises of the utopian imagination, which in my case led me to address questions of how better to manage, govern and develop curricula in schools.

Such positive imaginings or optimistic daydreams, which seek to relativize and offer a critique of the present by conjuring images of alternative futures, provide both an antidote to depressive inaction and a prompt to think progressively about and act for the better upon one's world.

References and other sources

This section provides full bibliographic details of all the sources referenced in the main text and other non-cited background material that informed different aspects of the book's various arguments.

Ackroyd, P. (1998) *The Life of Thomas More*, London, Chatto & Windus.

Adorno, T. (1974) The stars come down to earth: the *Los Angeles Times* astrology column, *Telos*, 19, 13–90.

Aitkenhead, D. (1998) The washing-machine salesmen of the third way are very common, *Guardian*, 18 September.

Alexander, P. and Gill, R. (eds) (1984) *Utopias*, London, Duckworth.

Anderson, P. (1994) Power, politics and the enlightenment. In Miliband, D. (ed.) *Reinventing the Left*, Cambridge, Polity Press.

Aquinas, T. (1952) *The Summa Theologica*, Chicago, William Benton (first published in the 13th century).

Armytage, W.H.G. (1961*) Heavens Below: Utopian Experiments in England, 1560–1960*, London, Routledge & Kegan Paul.

Aronson, R. (1999) Hope after hope?, *Social Research*, 66(2), 471–94.

Bailey, J. (1988) *Optimism*, London, Routledge.

Baker-Smith, D. (1991) *More's Utopia*, New York, HarperCollins.

Ball, S.J. (1990) *Politics and Policy Making in Education: Explorations in Policy Sociology*, London, Routledge.

Barnett, A. (1997) *This Time: Our Constitutional Revolution*, London, Vintage Books.

Bartkowski, F. (1989) *Feminist Utopias*, Lincoln, University of Nebraska Press.

Bauman, Z. (1973) *Culture as Praxis*, London, Routledge & Kegan Paul.

Bauman, Z. (1976) *Socialism: The Active Utopia*, London, George Allen & Unwin.

Bauman, Z. (1992) *Intimations of Postmodernity*, London, Routledge.

Bauman, Z. (1998) *Globalization: The Human Consequences*, Cambridge, Polity Press.

Beck, U. (1992) *Risk Society: Towards a New Modernity*, London, Sage.

Beck, U. (1997) *The Reinvention of Politics: Rethinking Modernity in the Global Social Order*, Cambridge, Polity Press.

Beck, U. (1998) *Democracy Without Enemies*, Cambridge, Polity Press.

Beck, U. and Beck-Gernsheim, E. (2002) *Individualization*, London, Sage.

Beecher, J. and Bienvenue, R. (1972) *The Utopian Vision of Charles Fourier: Selected Texts*, London, Jonathan Cape.

Benjamin, A. (1997) *Present Hope: Philosophy, Architecture, Judaism*, London, Routledge.

Benjamin, W. (1973) *Illuminations*, London, Fontana/Collins.

Bennett, O. (2001) *Cultural Pessimism: Narratives of Decline in the Postmodern World*, Edinburgh, Edinburgh University Press.

Bentley, T. (1998) *Learning Beyond the Classroom: Education for a Changing World*, London and New York, Routledge.

Benton, T. (1999) Radical politics – neither left nor right? In O'Brien, M., Penna, S. and Hay, C. (eds) *Theorizing Modernity: Reflexivity, Environment and Identity in Giddens' Social Theory*, London, Longman.

Berlin, I. (1991) *The Crooked Timber of Humanity: Chapters in the History of Ideas*, London, Fontana.

Bewes, T. (1997) *Cynicism and Postmodernity*, London, Verso.

Blair, T. (1998) Introduction. In *Bringing Britain Together: A National Strategy for Neighbourhood Renewal*, London, Stationery Office.

Bleich, D. (1984) *Utopia: The Psychology of a Cultural Fantasy*, Ann Arbor, MI, UMI Press.

Bloch, E. (1986) *The Principle of Hope* (Volumes 1 and 2), Oxford, Blackwell.

Bobbio, N. (1987) *The Future of Democracy: A Defence of the Rules of the Game*, Cambridge, Polity Press.

Boym, S. (2002) *The Future of Nostalgia*, New York, Basic Books.

Brighouse, H. (forthcoming, 2003) Against privatizing schools in the United Kingdom, *London Review of Education*, 1, 1.

Buber, M. (1958) *Paths in Utopia*, Boston, MA, Beacon Press.

Budge, I. (1996) *The New Challenge of Direct Democracy*, Cambridge, Polity Press.

Bush, T. and Middlewood, D. (eds) (1997) *Managing People in Education*, London, Paul Chapman.

Byers, S. (1998) Towards the third way in education. Lecture given at the Social Market Foundation, London, 1 July.

Caldwell, B.J. and Spinks, J.M. (1992) *Leading the Self-Managing School*, London, Falmer.

Campbell, R.J. and St. J. Neill, S.R. (1994) *Secondary Teachers at Work*, London, Routledge.

Carey, J. (ed.) (1999) *The Faber Book of Utopias*, London, Faber.

Carr, W. and Hartnett, A. (1996) *Education and the Struggle for Democracy: The Politics of Educational Ideas*, Buckingham, Open University Press.

Castells, E. (1996) *The Rise of the Network Society*, Oxford, Blackwell.

Catholic Education Service (1997) *The Common Good in Education*, London, Catholic Education Service.

Chambers, R.W. (1935) *Thomas More*, Harmondsworth, Penguin.

Chitty, C. and Simon, B. (1993) *Education Answers Back: Critical Responses to Government Policy*, London, Lawrence & Wishart.

Claeys, G. and Sargent, L.T. (eds) (1999) *The Utopian Reader*, New York, New York University Press.

Clews-Harrison, J.F. (1969) *Utopianism and Education: Robert Owen and the Owenites,* New York, Teachers College Press.

Cohen, J. and Rogers, J. (1995) Secondary associations and democratic governance. In Wright, E.O. (ed.) *Associations and Democracy: The Real Utopias Project* (Volume 1), London, Verso.

Coleman, J.S. (1988) Social capital in the creation of human capital, *American Journal of Sociology*, 94 (Supplement), 595–120.

Collinson, V., Killeavy, M. and Stephenson, H. (1999) Hope as a factor in teachers' thinking and classroom practice. Paper presented at the Annual Conference of the European Educational Research Association, Finland, 24–26 September.

Coyne, R. (1999) *Technoromanticism: Digital Narrative, Holism and the Romance of the Real*, Cambridge, MA, MIT Press.

Crick, B. (1964) *In Defence of Politics*, Harmondsworth, Penguin.

Dauenhauer, B.P. (1986) *The Politics of Hope*, New York, Routledge & Kegan Paul.

Deem, R., Brehony, R. and Heath, S. (1995) *Active Citizenship and the Governing of Schools*, Buckingham, Open University Press.

Deneen, Y. (1999) The politics of hope and optimism: Rorty, Havel and the democratic faith of John Dewey, *Social Research*, 6(2), 577–609.

Department for Education and Employment (DfEE) (1998) £75 million boosts radical education action zones to raise standards, *DfEE Press Release*, 23 June.

Department for Education and Skills (DfES) (UK) (2001a) *Education Action Zones: Annual Report*, 2000–2001, London, DfES.

Department for Education and Skills (DfES) (UK) (2001b) *Ofsted Inspections of the First Six Education Action Zones*, London, DfES.

Desroche, H. (1979) *The Sociology of Hope*, London, Routledge & Kegan Paul.

Dewey, J. (1963) *Democracy and Education*, New York, Macmillan (first published in 1916).

Dickson, M., Halpin, D., Power, S., Gewirtz, S., Whitty, G. and Telford, D. (2001) Education action zones and democratic participation, *School Leadership and Management*, 21(2), 169–81.

Eagleton, T. (1996) *The Illusions of Postmodernism*, Oxford, Blackwell.

Eagleton, T. (2000a) Utopia and its opposites. In Panitch, L. and Leys, C. (eds) *Necessary and Unnecessary Utopias*, Rendlesham, Merlin Press.

Eagleton, T. (2000b) *The Idea of Culture*, Oxford, Blackwell.

Earley, P., Evans, J., Collarbone, P., Gold, A. and Halpin, D. (2002) *Establishing the Current State of School Leadership in England* (Research Report 336), London, DfES.

Eco, U. (1981) *The Role of the Reader: Explorations in the Semiotics of Texts*, London, Hutchinson.

Edwards, G. (2000) Personal communication, 21 November.

Elliott, G. (2001) *Lifelong Learning: The Politics of the New Learning Environment*, London, Jessica Kingsley.

Evans, L. (1998) *Teacher Morale, Job Satisfaction and Motivation*, London, Paul Chapman.

Field, J. (2002) *Lifelong Learning and the New Educational Order*, Stoke on Trent, Trentham Books.

Fishman, R. (1984) Utopia in three dimensions: the ideal city and the origins of modern design. In Alexander, P. and Gill, R. (eds) *Utopias*, London, Duckworth.

Flax, J. (1990) *Psychoanalysis, Feminism and Postmodernism in the Contemporary West*, Berkeley, University of California Press.

Follett, M. (1926) *The New State: Group Organization as the Solution of Popular Government*, New York, Longman.

Foucault, M. (1970) *The Order of Things: An Archaeology of the Human Sciences*, London, Tavistock.

Foucault, M. (1998) Different spaces. In Fabion, J. (ed.) *Michel Foucault: The Essential Works* (Volume 2: Aesthetics), London, Penguin.

Fox, A. (1982) *Thomas More: History and Providence*, Oxford, Blackwell.

Freire, P. (1997) *Pedagogy of Hope*, New York, Continuum.

Fuchs, V. and Reklis, D. (1997) Mathematical achievement in eighth grade: inter-state and racial differences. *NBER Working Paper 4784*, Stanford, CA, NBER.

Fukuyama, F. (1995) *Trust: The Social Virtues and the Creation of Prosperity*, London, Hamish Hamilton.

Furstenberg, Q. and Hughes, M. (1995) Social capital and successful development among at-risk youth, *Journal of Marriage and the Family*, 57, 580–92.

Furukawa, H. (1989) Motivation to work. In Riches, C. and Morgan, C. (eds) *Human Resource Management in Schools*, Milton Keynes, Open University Press.

Gadamer, H-G. (1975) *Truth and Method*, London, Sheed & Ward.

Gambetta, D. (1998) 'Claro!': an essay on discursive machismo. In Elster, J. (ed.) *Deliberative Democracy*, Cambridge, Cambridge University Press.

Gardner, J. and Oswald, A. (1999) The determinants of job satisfaction in Britain. Working Paper, Coventry, Department of Economics, University of Warwick.

Geus, M. de (1999) *Ecological Utopias: Envisioning the Sustainable Society*, Utrecht, International Books.

Gewirtz, S. (1998) Education policy in urban areas: making sense of action zones. Paper presented to the Annual Conference of the Social Policy Association, University of Lincolnshire and Humberside, 14–16 July.

Gewirtz, S., Halpin, D., Power, S. and Whitty, G. (1998) The 'Third Way' starts off on a test drive, *Parliamentary Brief*, 5(7), 21–2.

Giddens, A. (1979) *Central Problems in Social Theory*, London, Macmillan.

Giddens, A. (1990) *The Consequences of Modernity*, Cambridge, Polity.

Giddens, A. (1991) *Modernity and Self-Identity: Self and Society in the Late Modern Age*, Cambridge, Polity Press.

Giddens, A. (1992) *The Transformation of Intimacy: Sexuality, Love and Eroticism in Modern Societies*, Cambridge, Polity Press.

Giddens, A. (1994) *Beyond Left and Right: The Future of Radical Politics*, Cambridge, Polity Press.

Giddens, A. (1996) *In Defence of Sociology: Essays, Interpretations and Rejoinders*, Cambridge, Polity Press.

Giddens, A. (1998) *The Third Way: The Renewal of Social Democracy*, Cambridge, Polity Press.

Giroux, H. (1988) *Teachers as Intellectuals: Toward a Critical Pedagogy of Learning*, New York, Bergin & Garvey.

Godfrey, J.J. (1987) *A Philosophy of Human Hope*, Dordrecht, The Netherlands, Martinus Nijhoff.

Goleman, D. (1996) *Emotional Intelligence*, London, Bloomsbury.

Goodwin, B. (ed.) (2000) *The Philosophy of Utopia*, London, Frank Cass.

Goodwin, B. and Taylor, K. (1982) *The Politics of Utopia: A Study in Theory and Practice*, London, Hutchinson.

Gorz, A. (1999) *Reclaiming Work: Beyond the Wage-Based Society*, Cambridge, Polity Press.

Grace, G. (1994) Urban education and the culture of contentment: the politics, culture and economics of inner-city schooling. In Stromquist, N.P. (ed.) *Education in Urban Areas*, Westport, CT, Praeger.

Gramsci A. (1992) *Prison Notebooks* (Volume 1), New York, Columbia State University.

Grayling, A.C. (2001) The last word on hope. In Grayling, A.C. (ed.) *The Meaning of Things*, London, Weidenfeld & Nicolson.

Grint, K. (1995) *Management: A Sociological Introduction*, Cambridge, Polity Press.

Grint, K. and Hogan, E. (1993) *Fatalism and Utopianism: Constructing an Index of Possibilities*, Oxford, Centre for Management Studies, Templeton College.

Gronn, P. (1999) *The Making of Educational Leaders*, London, Cassell.

Guy, J. (2000) *Thomas More*, London, Arnold.

Habermas, J. (1984) *The Theory of Communicative Action. Volume 1: Reason and the Rationalisation of Society*, London, Heinemann.

Hall, S. (1998) The great moving nowhere show, *Marxism Today*, November/December, 9–14.

Hallgartin, J. and Watling, R. (2001) Buying power: the role of the private sector in education action zones, *School Leadership and Management*, 21(2), 143–57.

Halpern, D. and Mikosz, D. (eds) (1998) *The Third Way: Summary of the Nexus On-Line Discussion*, London, Nexus.

Halpin, D. (1997) *Utopian Ideals, Democracy and the Politics of Education*. Inaugural Professorial Lecture, London, Goldsmiths, University of London.

Halpin, D. (1999a) Sociologising the Third Way: the contribution of Anthony Giddens and the significance of his analysis for education, *Forum*, 41(2), 53–7.

Halpin, D. (1999b) Utopian realism and a new politics of education: developing a critical theory without guarantees, *Journal of Education Policy*, 14(4), 345–61.

Halpin, D. (1999c) Democracy, inclusive schooling and the politics of education, *International Journal of Inclusive Education*, 3(3), 225–38.

Halpin, D. (2001a) Hope, utopianism and educational management, *Cambridge Journal of Education*, 31(1), 103–18.

Halpin, D. (2001b) Utopianism and education: the legacy of Thomas More, *British Journal of Educational Studies*, 49(3), 299–315.

Halpin, D. (2001c) The nature of hope and its significance for education, *British Journal of Educational Studies*, 49(4), 392–410.

Halpin, D. and Moore, A. (2000) Maintaining, reconstructing and creating tradition in education, *Oxford Review of Education*, 26(2), 133–44.

Hardy, D. (2000) *Utopian England: Community Experiments, 1900–1945*, London, E. & F. N. Spon.

Hargreaves, I. and Christie, I. (1998) *Tomorrow's Politics: The Third Way and Beyond*, London, Demos.

Harrison, J.F.C. (1969) *Utopianism and Education: Robert Owen and the Owenites*, New York, Teachers College Press.

Hartley, D. (1999) Marketing and the 're-enchantment' of school management, *British Journal of Sociology of Education*, 20(3), 309–24.

Harvey, D. (1996) *Justice, Nature and the Geography of Difference*, Oxford, Blackwell.

Harvey, D. (2000) *Spaces of Hope*, Edinburgh, Edinburgh University Press.

Hatcher, R. (1998) Labour, official school improvement and equality, *Journal of Education Policy*, 13(4), 485–500.

Havel, V. (1990) *Disturbing the Peace*, London, Faber & Faber.

Heidegger, M. (1962) *Being and Time*, Oxford, Blackwell.

Henry, C. (1990) *Culture and African-American Politics*, Bloomington, IN, Indiana University Press.

Hicks, D. (1998) Stories of hope: a response to the 'psychology of despair', *Environmental Education Research*, 4(2), 165–76.

Hirst, P. (1993) Associational democracy. In Held, D. (ed.) *Prospects for Democracy*, Cambridge, Polity Press.

Hirst, P. (1994) *Associative Democracy: New Forms of Economic and Social Governance*, Cambridge, Polity Press.

Hirst, P. (1997) *From Statism to Pluralism: Democracy, Civil Society and Global Politics*, London, University College London Press.

Hobsbawm, E. (1983) Inventing traditions. In Hobsbawm, E. and Ranger, T. (eds) *The Invention of Tradition*, Cambridge, Cambridge University Press.

Hobsbawm, E. (1998) The death of neo-liberalism, *Marxism Today*, November/ December, pp. 4–8.

Hodge, M. (1998) A pragmatic ideology, *Times Educational Supplement*, 12 June, p. 15.

Hogan, E. (n.d.) Women on the edge of genre: making utopian fiction work in feminist theory and practice. Unpublished paper, Templeton College, University of Oxford.

Hogan, P. (1996) Forlorn hopes and great expectations: teaching as a way of life in an age of uncertainty, *Irish Educational Studies*, 16 (Spring), 1–18.

Holmes, G. (1993) *Essential School Leadership: Developing Vision and Purpose in Management*, London, Kogan Page.

Hutton, W. (1998) Editorial, *Sunday Observer*, 20 September, p. 30.

Ignatieff, M. (1994) *The Needs of Strangers*, London, Vintage Books.

Jacoby, R. (2000) *The End of Utopia: Politics and Culture in an Age of Apathy*, London, Basic Books.

Jacques, M. (1998) Good to be back, *Marxism Today*, November/December, pp. 2–3.

Johnson, J. (1998) Arguing for deliberation: some sceptical considerations. In Elster, J. (ed.) *Deliberative Democracy*, Cambridge, Cambridge University Press.

Judd, J. (1998) Action zones set schools tough targets, *Independent*, 19 September.

Kandinsky, W. (1982) 'And': Some remarks on synthetic art. In Lindsay, K. and Vergo, P. (eds) *Kandinsky's Complete Writings on Art*, Volume 2 (1992– 1943), Boston, University of Boston Press.

Kant, I. (1978) *Critique of Pure Reason*, London, Macmillan (first published 1781).

Kast, V. (1991) *Joy, Inspiration and Hope*, College Station, Tx, Texas A&M University Press.

Keane, J. (1988) *Democracy and Civil Society*, London, Verso.

Kenny, A. (1983) *Thomas More*, Oxford, Oxford University Press.

Kinney, A. F. (1979) *Rhetoric and Poetic in Thomas More's Utopia*, New York, Malibu.

Kolnai, A. (1995) *The Utopian Mind and Other Papers*, London, Athlone Press.

Kumar, K. (1991) *Utopianism*, Milton Keynes, Open University Press.

Kumar, K. (1993) The end of socialism? The end of utopia? In Kumar, K. and Bann, S. (eds.) *Utopias and the Millennium*, London, Reaktion Books.

Labour Party (1997) *Education Action Zones: Labour's Proposals to Raise Standards in Schools*, London, Labour Party.

Lasch, C. (1991) *The True and Only Heaven: Progress and its Critics*, New York, Norton & Co.

Lawton, D. (1975) *Class, Culture and the Curriculum*, London, Routledge and Kegan Paul.

Lazarus, R.S. and Lazarus, B.N. (1994) *Passion and Reason: Making Sense of our Emotions*, Oxford, Oxford University Press.

Levitas, R. (1990a) *The Concept of Utopia*, London, Philip Allan.

Levitas, R. (1990b) Educated hope: Ernst Bloch on abstract and concrete utopia, *Utopian Studies*, 1(2), 13–26.

Levitas, R. (1993) The future of thinking about the future. In Bird, J., Curtis, B., Putman, T., Roberston, G. and Tickner, L. (eds) *Mapping the Futures: Local Cultures, Global Change*, London, Routledge.

Levitas, R. (2001a) Against work: a utopian incursion into social policy, *Critical Social Policy*, 21(4), 449–65.

Levitas, R. (2001) For utopia: the (limits of the) utopian function in late capitalist society. In Goodwin, B. (ed.) *The Philosophy of Utopia*, London, Frank Cass.

Liston, D.P. (2000) Love and despair in teaching, *Educational Theory*, 50(1), 81–102.

Longworth, N. and Davies, W.K. (1996) *Lifelong Learning*, London, Kogan Page.

Ludema, J.D. (2000) From deficit discourse to vocabularies of hope: the power of appreciation. In Cooperrider, D., Sorenson, P.F., Whitney, D. and Yaeger, T.F. (eds) *Appreciative Enquiry: Rethinking Human Organization Towards a Positive Theory of Change*, Champaigne, IL, Stipes Publishing.

Ludema, J.D., Wilmot, T.B. and Srivastva, S. (1997) Organizational hope: reaffirming the constructive task of social and organizational inquiry, *Human Relations*, 50(8), 1015–51.

Lynch, W.F. (1965) *Images of Hope*, Notre Dame, Notre Dame Press.

McKenna, E. (2001) *The Task of Utopia: A Pragmatist and Feminist Perspective*, Oxford, Rowan & Littlefield.

MacLeod, D. (1996) Stick to tradition, Charles tells teachers, *Guardian*, 12 July, p. 1.

MacQuarrie, J. (1966) *The Principles of Christian Theology*, London, SCM Press.

MacQuarrie, J. (1978) *Christian Hope*, London, SCM Press.

Mannheim, K. (1979) *Ideology and Utopia: An Introduction to the Sociology of Knowledge*, London, Routledge & Kegan Paul.

Mansbridge, J. (1991) Feminism and democratic community. In Chapman, J.W. and Shapiro, I. (eds) *Democratic Community*, New York, New York University Press.

Mansell, W. (2001) Private sector cold-shoulders fledgling EAZs, *Times Educational Supplement*, 27 July, p. 2.

Manseu, W. (2002) Action zones fail to help inner-city secondaries, *Times Educational Supplement*, 13 November, p. 17.

Marcel, G. (1951) *Homo Viator: Introduction to a Metaphysics of Hope*, London, Victor Gollancz.

Marcel, G. (1962) *The Philosophy of Existentialism*, New York, Citadel Press.

Marcel, G. (1965) *Being and Having*, London, Collins.

Marin, L. (1984) *Utopics: The Semiological Play of Textual Places*, Atlantic City, NJ, Humanities Press International.

Marin, L. (1993) The frontiers of utopia. In Kumar, K. and Bann, S. (eds) *Utopias and the Millennium*, London, Reaktion Books.

Marius, R. (1984) *Thomas More*, New York, Alfred A. Knopf.

Martin, J., Ranson, S., McKeown, P. and Nixon, J. (1996) School governance for the civil society: redefining the boundaries between schools and parents, *Local Government Studies*, 22(4), 210–28.

Martineau, A. (1986) *Herbert Marcuse's Utopia*, Montreal, Harvest House.

Midgley, M. (1996) *Utopias, Dolphins and Computers: Problems of Philosophical Plumbing*, London, Routledge.

Moltmann, J. (1967) *Theology of Hope: On the Ground and the Implications of Christian Eschatology*, London, SCM Press.

Moltmann, J. (1971) *Hope and Planning*, London, SCM Press.

Moore, A., Edwards, G., Halpin, D. and George, R. (2002) Compliance, resistance and pragmatism: the (re)construction of school teacher identities in a period of intensive educational reform, *British Educational Research Journal*, 28(4), 551–66.

Mouffe, C. (1998) The radical centre: a politics without adversary, *Soundings*, 9 (summer), 11–23.

Moylan, T. (1986) *Demand the Impossible: Science Fiction and the Utopian Imagination*, London, Methuen.

Murdoch, I. (1970) *The Sovereignty of Good*, London, Routledge & Kegan Paul.

Murphy, A. (1996) *Thomas More*, London, Fount Books.

Nanus, B. (1992) *Visionary Leadership*, San Francisco, CA, Jossy-Bass.

Nesse, R.M. (1999) The evolution of hope and despair, *Social Research*, 66(2), 429–69.

Nixon, J., Martin, J., McKeown, P. and Ranson, S. (1996) *Encouraging Learning: Towards a Theory of the Learning School*, Buckingham, Open University Press.

Nixon, J., Martin, J., McKeown, P. and Ranson, S. (1997a) Towards a learning profession: changing codes of occupational practice within the new management of education, *British Journal of Sociology of Education*, 18(1), 5–28.

Nixon, J., Martin, J., McKeown, P. and Ranson, S. (1997b) Confronting 'failure': towards a pedagogy of recognition, *International Journal of Inclusive Education*, 1(2), 121–41.

Nozick, R. (1974) *Anarchy, State and Utopia*, Oxford, Blackwell.

Olin, J.C. (ed.) (1989) *Interpreting Thomas More's Utopia*, New York, Fordham.

Panitch, L. and Leys, C. (eds) (2000) *Necessary and Unnecessary Utopias*, Rendlesham, The Merlin Press.

Parker, M. (ed.) (2002) *Utopia and Organization*, Oxford, Blackwell.

Phillips, A. (1993) *Democracy and Difference*, Cambridge, Polity Press.

Phillips, A. (1995) *The Politics of Presence*, Oxford, Oxford University Press.

Plattel, M. (1972) *Utopian and Critical Thinking*, Pittsburgh, PA, Duquesne University Press.

Plewis, I. (1998) Inequalities, targets and zones, *New Economy*, 5(2), 104–08.

Popper, K. (1961) *Conjectures and Refutations: The Growth of Scientific Knowledge*, London, Routledge & Kegan Paul.

Power, S. and Whitty, G. (1999) New Labour's education policy: first, second or third way? *Journal of Education Policy*, 14(5), 535–46.

Purkey, W.W. and Novak, J. (1990) *Inviting School Success*, Belmont, CA, Wadsworth.

Putman, R.D. with Leonardi, R. and Nanetti, R.Y. (1993) *Making Democracy Work: Civic Traditions in Modern Italy*, Princeton, NJ, Princeton University Press.

Quicke, J. (1999) *Curriculum for Life: Schools for a Democratic Learning Society*, Buckingham, Open University Press.

Rafferty, F. (1998) Action zones will pilot new ideas, *Times Educational Supplement*, 6 February, p. 4.

Ranson, S. (1994) *Towards the Learning Society*, London, Cassell.

Ranson, S. (2000) Recognizing the pedagogy of voice in a learning community, *Educational Management and Administration*, 28(3), 263–79.

Ranson, S. and Stewart, J. (1998) Citizenship in the public domain for trust in civil society. In Coulson, A. (ed.) *Trust and Contracts*, London, Policy Press.

Reich, R. (1998) Light the blue touch paper, *Sunday Observer*, 15 March.

Reynolds, J. and Skilbeck, M. (1976) *Culture and the Classroom*, London, Open Books.

Riches, C. (1997) Managing for people and performance. In Bush, T. and Middlewood, D. (eds) (1997) *Managing People in Education*, London, Paul Chapman.

Riches, C. and Morgan, C (eds) (1989) *Human Resource Management in Schools*, Milton Keynes, Open University Press.

Riley, K., Watling, R., Rowles, D. and Hopkins, D (1998) *Education Action Zones: Some Lessons Learned from the First Wave of Applications*, London, The London Network.

Rorty, R. (1989) *Contingency, Irony and Solidarity*, Cambridge, Cambridge University Press.

Rorty, R. (1998) *Achieving Our Country*, Cambridge, MA, Harvard University Press.

Rorty, R. (1999) *Philosophy and Social Hope*, Harmondsworth, Penguin.

Ruskin, J. (1898) (12th edn) *Unto this Last: Four Essays on the First Principles of Political Economy*, Croydon, George Allen.

Sacks, J. (1997) *The Politics of Hope*, London, Jonathan Cape.

Sacks, J. (2002) *The Dignity of Difference: How to Avoid the Clash of Civilizations*, London, Continuum.

Sargent, L.T. (1982) Authority and utopia: utopianism in political context, *Polity*, 14(4), 565–84.

Sargent, L.T. (1994) The three faces of utopianism revisited, *Utopian Studies*, 5(1), 1–37.

Sargisson, L. (1996) *Contemporary Feminist Utopias*, London, Routledge.

Schmitter, P.C. (1995) The irony of modern democracy and the viability of efforts to reform its practice. In Wright, E.O. (ed.) *Associations and Democracy: The Real Utopias Project* (Volume 1), London, Verso.

Seltzer, K. and Bentley, T. (1999) *The Creative Age: Knowledge and Skills for the New Economy*, London, Demos.

Simecka, M. (1984) A world with utopias or without them? In Alexander, P. and Gill, R. (eds) *Utopias*, London, Duckworth.

Skidelski, R.and Raymond, K. (1998) *Education Action Zones: The Conditions of Success*, London, Social Market Foundation.

Skilbeck, M. (1976) The curriculum as a cultural map. In *Culture, Ideology and Knowledge*, Units 3 and 4 of the Open University Course E203 Curriculum Design and Development, Milton Keynes, Open University Press.

Sloterdijk, P. (1997) *Critique of Cynical Reason*, London, Verso.

Smithers, R. (1999) Teachers turn their backs on the classroom, *Guardian*, 9 September, p. 6.

Socialist Teachers Alliance (1998) *Trojan Horses – Education Action Zones: The Case Against the Privatization of Education*, London, Socialist Teachers Alliance.

Soper, K. (1993) Postmodernism, subjectivity and the question of value. In Squires, J. (ed.) *Principled Positions: Postmodernism and the Rediscovery of Value*, London, Lawrence & Wishart.

Soros, G. (1998) *The Crisis of Global Capitalism: Open Society Endangered*, London, Little Brown.

Squires, J. (ed.) *Principled Positions: Postmodernism and the Rediscovery of Value*, London, Lawrence & Wishart.

Stewart, J. (1996a) Innovation in democratic practice in local government, *Policy and Politics*, 24(1), 29–42.

Stewart, J. (1996b) Democracy and local government. In Hirst, P. and Khilnani, S. (eds) *Reinventing Democracy*, Oxford, Blackwell.

Stillman, P. G. (2001) 'Nothing is, but what is not', utopias as practice political philosophy. In Goodwin, B. (ed.) *The Philosophy of Utopia*, London, Frank Cass.

Stoll, L. and Fink, D. (1996) *Changing Our Schools: Linking School Effectiveness and School Improvement*, Buckingham, Open University Press.

Stotland, E. (1969) *The Psychology of Hope*, San Francisco, CA, Jossey-Bass.

Swords, D. (1999) Measuring the creativity climate. Paper presented at the Annual Conference of the Institute of Personnel and Development, Olympia, London, 13–15 April.

Tannen, D. (1992) *You Don't Understand: Women and Men in Conversation*, London, Virago Press.

Tannen, D. (1998) *The Argument Culture*, London, Virago Press.

Taylor, C. (1994) The politics of recognition. In Gutman, A. (ed.) *Multiculturalism: Examining the Politics of Recognition*, Princeton, NJ, University of Princeton Press.

Taylor, S.E. (1989) *Positive Illusions*, New York, Basic Books.

Tiger, L. (1985) *Optimism: The Biology of Hope*, London, Secker & Warburg

Tiger, L. (1999) Hope springs eternal, *Social Research*, 66(2), 611–23.

Tillich, P. (1971) The political meaning of utopia. In Tillich, P. (ed.) *Political Expectations*, New York, Harper & Row.

Turner, P. (1965) *Introduction to Thomas More's Utopia*, Harmondswoth, Penguin.

Varlaam, A., Nuttall, D. and Walker, A. (1992) *What Makes Teachers Tick?: A Survey of Teacher Morale and Motivation*, London, Centre for Educational Research, London School of Economics and Political Science.

Walsh, P. (1993) *Education and Meaning: Philosophy in Practice*, London, Cassell.

Warnock, M. (1986) The education of the emotions. In Cooper, D. (ed.) *Education, Values and the Mind*, London, Routledge.

Watkins, C., Carnell, E., Lodge, C., Wagner, P. and Whalley, C. (2002) *Effective Learning* (Research Matters No.17), London, University of London's Institute of Education.

Wegemer, G.B. (1995) *Thomas More: A Portrait of Courage*, Princeton, NJ, Scepter Publishers.

West, M. and Patterson, M. (1999) The productivity gap, *New Economy*, 6(1), 22–7.

Whitty, G. (1997) Social theory and education policy: the legacy of Karl Mannheim, *British Journal of Sociology of Education*, 18(2), 149–64.

Whitty, G., Power, S. and Halpin, D. (1998) *Devolution and Choice in Education: The School, the State and the Market*, Buckingham, Open University Press.

Wilde, O. (1894) The soul of man under socialism. Reissued in Wilde, O. (1986) *De Profundis and Other Writings*, Harmondsworth, Penguin.

Wilkinson, R.G. (1996) *Unhealthy Societies: The Afflictions of Inequality*, London, Routledge.

Williams, R. (1961) *Culture and Society 1780–1950*, Harmondsworth, Penguin.

Williams, R. (1965) *The Long Revolution*, Harmondsworth, Penguin.

Williams, R. (1977) *Marxism and Literature*, Oxford, Oxford University Press.

Williams, R. (1980) Utopia and science fiction. In Williams, R. (ed.) *Problems in Materialism and Culture*, London, Verso.

Williams, R. (1983) *Towards 2000*, London, Chatto & Windus.

Williams, R. (1989) *Resources of Hope*, London, Verso.

Willms, J.D. (1997) Quality and inequality in children's literacy: the effects of families, schools and communities. Mimeo, University of New Brunswick.

Wilson, B. and Corcoran, T. (1988) *Successful Secondary Schools: Visions of Excellence in American Public Education*, London, Falmer Press.

Wootton, D. (1999) *Edited Translation of Thomas More's Utopia*, Indianapolis, ID, Hackett Publishing.

Wright, E.O. (1995) Preface: The Real Utopias Project. In Cohen, J. and Rogers, J. (eds) *Associations and Democracy*, London, Verso.

Yeatman, A. (1994) *Postmodern Revisionings of the Political*, London, Routledge.

Young, I.M. (1996) Communication and the other: beyond deliberative democracy. In Benhabib, S. (ed.) *Democracy and Difference: Contesting the Boundaries of the Political*, Princeton, NJ, Princeton University Press.

Index